Gen Z @ Work

Gen Z @ Work

How the Next Generation Is Transforming the Workplace

DAVID STILLMAN AND
JONAH STILLMAN

An Imprint of HarperCollins*Publishers*

 For information, address HarperCollins Publishers, 195 Broadway, New York, NY 10007.

HarperCollins books may be purchased for educational, business, or sales promotional use. For information, please email the Special Markets Department at SPsales@harpercollins.com.

FIRST EDITION

Designed by Lucy Albanese
Emoji symbols on pages 98, 100, and 101: Shutterstock

Library of Congress Cataloging-in-Publication Data has been applied for.

ISBN: 978-0-06-247544-2

17 18 19 20 21 lsc 10 9 8 7 6 5 4 3 2 1

This book is dedicated to the late Allan Grosh. If anyone would be excited to see Gen Z show up at work, it would be you. They're missing out on a great mentor.

CONTENTS

Gen Z @ Work

INTRODUCTION

A new generation is starting to hit our workforce, yet no one seems to be talking about it. Until now.

Gen Z. Born 1995–2012.

Usually the first thing people think is, "Is that what we are calling them?" We can address the name later. In fact, it has its own chapter. For now let's run with it.

We may have thought about Gen Z as consumers and know how to sell them blue jeans or Barbie dolls. However, we have not thought about them as employees and what it will take to recruit, retain, manage, or motivate them.

The other thing most people are thinking: "Wait! Aren't they Millennials?"

No. They're not. In fact, they are quite different.

Believe it or not, Millennials have grown up. Beyoncé is no

longer a single lady—she's an entertainment mogul. Britney and Justin have broken up, moved on, and are even parents. In fact, according to *Time* magazine, 47 percent of Millennials are moms and dads. Millennials own houses, are done with the college phase, and have launched their careers. There is not a day that goes by where you don't hear something about the Millennials. The most talked-about generation in history. The problem is that we talk about them so much we can't imagine life *after* the Millennials.

We haven't thought about a different generation showing up at the office because it felt so far away. Also, more than just the Millennials, we are focused on the Baby Boomers, who are edging into retirement. We have to be sure all their knowledge and wisdom is captured before it's gone. Leaders are also busy still grooming and growing Xers (Gen Z's parents) to take over, a generation whom they have historically ignored or even avoided.

And now there is a whole new generation to get to know? Really?

Yes!

Introducing Gen Z. The leading edge is already in their twenties. At 72.8 million strong, Gen Z are making their presence known in the workplace and organizations and leaders cannot afford to ignore them. The risk in not getting to know Gen Z is that we will simply treat them like the Millennials. Big mistake and it's one that we've made before.

When Gen X showed up at work, no one paid attention. In fact, no one had given it any thought. What?! There's life *after* the Baby Boomers?! The Boomers garnered the limelight in every marketplace. The workplace spent countless hours designing and implementing rules and regulations, processes, and procedures to help navigate the 80 million Boomers competing to get ahead. It was all Baby Boomer, all the time. When Gen X showed up leaders tried to treat them like the Boomers and—KABOOM! Gen X was nothing like the Baby Boomers and from recruiting to career paths to communication and beyond, the workplace was flooded with costly gaps. Even today, companies can feel the pain.

Nothing can stop the arrival of a new generation. The time to get to know Gen Z is today.

However, when I introduce the dialogue about Gen Z hitting the workplace, most of the faces look shocked, mad, exhausted, or confused. They rarely look excited. I definitely sense a feeling of Millennial fatigue out there. As I mentioned, there isn't a day that goes by where we don't hear something about the Millennials. People are just tired of talking about a generation, which definitely does not bode well for Gen Z. However, as I share some results from our national surveys about Gen Z at work, I watch most faces go from mad, exhausted, or confused to relieved, excited, and definitely intrigued.

If anyone is going to be intrigued with a new generation, it's probably going to be me.

Allow me to introduce myself. My name is David Stillman.

I have spent close to twenty years researching, writing, and speaking to companies about the topic of generations. It was my full-time job for close to fifteen years. In the mid-1990s, I cofounded a business with a Baby Boomer named Lynne Lancaster. Lynne and I had met while working on a project together at our previous jobs and clashed like no one's business. However, we still liked each other. After the project was done, we went out to lunch to celebrate and talked about our generational differences. We quickly realized that if we were struggling to bridge generational gaps, others were as well. While there were a handful of generational experts out there focusing on a particular generation, we saw a need to pioneer the dialogue about what happens when we put these generations together—especially in the workplace.

We quit our jobs shortly after and started our company with the mission of helping Traditionalists, Baby Boomers, Gen Xers, and Millennials bridge the gaps in the workplace and marketplace. Our company took off. The topic was very popular as Xers were shaking up the workplace like never before. Everyone wanted to talk about it. Once we had collected enough primary research, we published our first book, *When Generations Collide.* We hit the speaking circuit with a vengeance, often speaking together or separately.

Lynne and I did more than just write and talk about the generations—we built a thriving company around our mission of bridging generational gaps. We created a train-the-trainer program, e-learning platform, and even a corporate entertainment show. As Millennials started to enter the workplace, we wrote and published our second book, *The M-Factor: How the Millennial Generation Is Rocking the Workplace.*

After more than a decade of being on the road, I was tired. Throw in three kids and a germ phobia, and the fun wears off. The opportunity came to sell our business and we took it.

I wasn't sure what I was going to do next when a dear friend and colleague, Marc Kielburger, came to town. He and his brother Craig, whom I met on an airplane, have cofounded the world's largest global youth empowerment movement—called WE. My family had supported one of their international programs in Kenya and had gotten to know their organization quite well. We traveled to Kenya multiple times to build schools, and our experiences with the Kielburgers have always been life changing. They were operating WE in eight countries around the world and were ready to bring their program to the United States. Marc knew I had sold my company and asked me to join a team of two others to spearhead their expansion into the States.

My first reaction was that I was not nice enough to work at a nonprofit. I can be quite opinionated, am known to speak my mind, and am not exactly the most patient. I had zero experience working for a nonprofit and other than helping my kids sell wrapping paper for their schools at holiday time, I hadn't done any fund-raising, either.

So, naturally, I took the job.

What I didn't realize was that I would be immersed right back into the generational dialogue. WE gave me my first opportunity to see and work with Gen Z. I was surrounded by incredible teenagers who were taking local and global action to make the world a better place. Collecting coins, doing car washes, bake sales, dance-a-thons, bike rides, hikes . . . mini businesses. I was so excited by their maturity, sense of self, willingness to work hard, and commitment to service. At the same time, I could see some scary gaps on the horizon as their independent nature would likely clash with collaborative Millennials.

Gen Z entering the workplace resonated even more with me as I have two Gen Z kids who are already working. My oldest daughter, nineteen-year-old Ellie, is a paid intern at the Minnesota Department of Education, and my seventeen-year-old son, Jonah, is my business partner. More on that later. My nine-year-old daughter, Sadie, has bigger plans of being the next singer-songwriter YouTube sensation. You'll be the first to know.

In many meetings with corporations to talk about supporting the WE program in the United States, they would refer to the youth as Millennials. Even Millennials themselves would call them that. However, the traits that I was seeing among Gen Z did not align with all the research and writing I had done on Millennials. My gut told me that Gen Z was going to be different than the Millennials and I also knew that if leaders didn't wake up to this fact, they would find themselves in trouble.

I knew I had to go on more than my gut, so I took the next step. I partnered with the Institute for Corporate Productivity (i4cp) to conduct two national surveys on Gen Z's workplace attitudes. We surveyed Gen Zers across the country who are 15–21 years old and focused all of the questions on their workplace attitudes. In addition to i4cp, I partnered with my son Jonah's high school business immersion program, called VANTAGE. These amazing Gen Zers collaborated with i4cp to figure out what questions to ask and how to get the survey out to their generation across the country. They were also instrumental in analyzing the results.

Speaking of results, my gut was confirmed. The national surveys proved that Gen Z was not at all like the Millennials. In fact, they were quite different. One thing was for sure: Gen Z is ready and eager to kick some serious butt at work. Careers are top of mind. Our study definitely revealed they are focused on and preparing for careers at a young age. On one hand, I could see how excited Gen Z was to dive into their careers, while on the other, I saw that employers were not even thinking about them and don't realize that so many workplace practices are about to need another overhaul.

This really propelled my interest in pioneering another dialogue. I started to talk about it all the time at home with my Gen Z kids. Rather than roll their eyes at me, they really engaged in the dialogue. But of course they did . . . at last I was talking about *their* generation.

Then, one night before going to bed, my Gen Z son Jonah asked me a question.

"Dad, do you think I could be the voice of my generation?"

Have you ever had a moment in your life where the idea lightbulb goes off above your head and you just know deep down that the idea is a good one?

The lightbulb went off for me big-time.

Jonah could help me introduce Gen Z. It's more authentic coming from him. He could discuss who Gen Z is, and I could rely on my years of studying the generations to talk about what it means for the rest of us. It just felt right.

Jonah and I started with a few test speeches and the next thing we knew, we had a website, logo, an app, offerings, and basically a new business. We called it Gen Z Guru. We wanted to start by pioneering a dialogue about Gen Z at work. We had great data and knew leaders weren't talking about Gen Z.

We even traveled to two presidential primaries to talk about the Gen Z vote.

Running a business with Jonah, I quickly noticed how different we were. It was déjà vu, reminding me of when Lynne and I opened our business. I started to collect stories of working together, along with case studies and results from our national surveys, and it wasn't long before the topic of writing a book came about.

Why Jonah? First, so my other kids don't end up on Dr. Phil's couch, I of course love all of them the same. But Ellie's already in college and off on her own amazing pursuit for a career in education and Sadie's only interest in attending a generations presentation would be if she could sing the national anthem.

Jonah is a natural. He is passionate about Gen Z. His comfort level with getting up and talking in front of a crowd is impressive. He's got guts. He has been hearing about the generations since he was born. From the get-go, I have been so impressed by his willingness to work hard and do what it takes to prepare speeches and write this book. He even gave up his lifelong passion, which he can explain. He is one dedicated kid.

Most important, he truly gets the golden rule of the generations. He knows that no generation is better, worse, right, or wrong . . . they are just different. I know that as passionate as he is to introduce Gen Z to the other generations, he is equally as excited to learn about them.

Best of all, we are blessed with an awesome relationship. Jonah and I get along great. We have a lot in common. This is actually a big trend with Gen Z and their Gen X parents we talk more about in this book. For the first time in history, parents and kids are sharing playlists, hobbies, and even clothes. All said, there is no denying who is the boss.

This is the part where I stop to give a big shout-out to Jonah's principal and teachers, who have been nothing but supportive. Another shout-out to those pioneering companies and individuals who early on brought us in to start the dialogue about Gen Z.

If you're reading this book for parenting advice, I'm not so sure I'm your guy. My kids eat sugared cereal, don't have real bedtimes, and I've taught them that there is such a thing as a dumb question. However, you will definitely get many insights into your Gen Z kids and how they will be as employees.

But that's just the Xers. For all the Boomer and Millennial readers, odds are they don't have as many Gen Zers in their lives.

This book is about Gen Z at work. The goal is to pioneer a dialogue about what they will be like in the workplace. We want to introduce you to who they are and why, and their seven key traits:

1. **Phigital:** Gen Z is the first generation born into a world where every physical aspect (people and places) has a digital equivalent. For Gen Z, the real world and the virtual world naturally overlap. Virtual is simply part of their reality. The world of work has typically been slow to adapt to digital solutions and will be challenged like never before when it comes to finding its place in the phigital world. Ninety-one percent of Gen Z say that a company's technological sophistication would impact their decision to work there.

2. **Hyper-Custom:** Gen Z has always worked hard at identifying and customizing their own brand for the world to know. Their ability to customize everything has created an expectation that there is an intimate understanding of their behaviors and desires. From job titles to career paths, the pressure to customize has been turned up. This is going to be tough for the world of work, which has historically focused on trying to be fair and treating everyone the same. Fifty-six percent of Gen Z would rather write their own job description than be given a generic one.

3. **Realistic:** Growing up during the aftermath of 9/11, with terrorism part of everyday life, as well as living through a severe recession early on, has created a very

pragmatic mindset when it comes to planning and preparing for the future. Colleges and universities were the first to struggle with this realistic attitude and the workplace is next. With idealistic Millennials as their frontline managers, the potential for gaps with Gen Z is huge. As Gen Z sees it, if you're going to survive or even thrive, you'd better get real about what it's going to take.

4. **FOMO:** Gen Z suffers from an intense fear of missing out on anything. The good news is that they will stay on top of all trends and competition. The bad news is that Gen Z will always worry that they aren't moving ahead fast enough and in the right direction. The workplace will be challenged by Gen Z, who will want to have a lot in the hopper at all times to be sure they aren't missing out. Seventy-five percent of Gen Z would be interested in a situation in which they could have multiple roles within one place of employment.

5. **Weconomists:** From Uber to Airbnb, Gen Z has only known a world with a shared economy. Gen Z will push the workplace to break down internal and external silos to leverage the collective in new convenient and cost-effective ways. More than just as employees, Gen Z will leverage the power of "we" in their role as philanthropists. Gen Z will expect to partner with their employers to fix the wrongs they are seeing in the world. Ninety-three percent of Gen Z says that a company's impact on society affects their decision to work there.

6. **DIY:** Gen Z is the do-it-yourself generation. Having grown up with YouTube, which can teach them how to do just about anything, Gen Z believes that they can do just about anything themselves. On top of that, they have been encouraged by their independent Gen X parents not to follow traditional paths. Gen Z is fiercely independent and will collide head-on with so many of the collaborative cultures that Millennials have fought for. Seventy-one percent of Gen Z said they believe the phrase "if you want it done right, then do it yourself!"

7. **Driven:** With parents who drilled into them that participation is not a real award and that there are winners and losers, a recession that pulled the rug out from their predecessors, and a rate of change that is hard to keep up with, it is no wonder that Gen Z is one driven generation. Gen Z is ready and hungry to roll up their sleeves. They will be more competitive as well as private than previous generations. Pressure will be on for companies to convince Gen Z that they are the winning team. Seventy-two percent of Gen Z said they are competitive with people doing the same job.

By understanding the seven traits, we can learn about what they are looking for in their careers. Where might we clash with Gen Z? Where will we click?

We have a whole new generation hitting our workplace. It doesn't happen that often. For many of you, it will be the last generation you have to worry about getting to know at work. For the rest, it will be the first time you've welcomed a new generation and, scary to think, it won't be the last. Millennials' kids will be here before we know it.

So if you haven't put the book down by now, keep reading. Get to know Gen Z. You won't get a second chance to make a first impression.

And come to think of it . . . neither will they.

No pressure, Jonah.

Hi. My name is Jonah Stillman and I am seventeen years old. If there are any Gen Z readers, no doubt you've moved on. Our eight-second attention span likely has you skipping the intro and just diving into the first chapter. But for the other generations of readers . . . I am a classic Gen Zer. I love Snapchat and Twitter and think email is for my parents' generation. Most of my entertainment is consumed on a cell phone or laptop and if a video is longer than thirty seconds, there's a good chance I'm hitting delete. I came out of the womb ready to go as my hobbies pretty much include anything that involves action. My biggest passion has been alpine snowboarding. Since the age of six, I have competed at the national level, even bringing home the bronze one year.

I go to a really big high school that I like a lot. There are approximately 700 students in my class and 3,200 in the whole school. My favorite part of school is that I am part of a program called VANTAGE. It's an immersive business program. Here's the elevator pitch—why just sit in class and learn AP economics and IB business when you can actually apply it by doing real-world projects for companies? Half of my day I spend with other students off campus in an officelike environment and work on projects for companies like General Mills. As talked about in this book, programs like this are perfect for my generation since we are really focused on understanding how what we learn in school actually applies to our future.

My parents turned me on to volunteering at a young age. I remember I was nine years old when my dad left for three weeks to build schools in Kenya. He came home and told me about how kids play soccer on a slanted field with holes and rocks. I decided I wanted to do something about it so I teamed up with my cousin Jacob and we raised enough money to build a proper soccer field. Four years later, my dad brought me with him to Kenya, where I got to cut the ribbon on the soccer field. I've also been lucky to travel to Ecuador on a summer program to build schools and set up clean water programs. Like many Gen Zers, giving back is just part of my DNA.

I've grown up listening to my dad talk about the generations. Every year, each kid got to go with him to a conference that was in a great location—usually Disney. As much as we went with him for the chance to hit the pool or rides, I always loved going with him to hear him speak. I never got tired of listening to him talk passionately about the topic and especially about his generation. I always wondered when he would talk about my generation.

When he started to talk about Gen Z, I was interested. One thing about my dad is that when he has an idea . . . he's *all* in. Buckle up. Ideation mode with my dad can be part exciting, part chaotic, and yes . . . a little psychotic. We talked about Gen Z in the car, on a chairlift, or at breakfast, lunch, or dinner. However, the more my dad talked about it, the more I got excited. As the data proved how different we were from the Millennials, I too saw a need. Someone had to introduce the world to Gen Z.

So off went my lightbulb and I said to my dad, "Dad, do you think I could be the voice of my generation?"

I'm sure there will be lots of Gen Z experts and speakers out there. There will never be one voice of Gen Z, but there is something to trying to be one of the first to put it on the radar. However, from conducting primary research to learning how to deliver a keynote speech to fine-tuning my writing skills (I am the king of run-on sentences), I quickly learned that being the voice of my generation was going to be a lot of work. Throw in homework and studying for the ACT, and I also quickly became overwhelmed. I really felt the need to spread the word about Gen Z and couldn't stop thinking about it. So, after ten years of competing at alpine snowboarding, I decided to give it up. Not an easy decision, and I often found myself missing my time on the slopes.

Which brings me to running a business with my dad. We bump heads on a lot of things—many of which are clearly generational. It's so cool to witness firsthand when a gap between a Gen Zer and Gen Xer is bridged and it's so painful when the gap seems to only get larger. If a father and son can have these collisions at home, I can only imagine what it will be like at work. These are the stories we try to share throughout the book . . . of course, along with all of the research.

As for research, it was fascinating for me to share results with my peers, who quickly joined me in wanting to make sure businesses and their leaders knew that we were different. On a very small scale, I felt like I was starting a movement. I knew we were on to something.

As my dad and I started to give speeches to share the data with companies, my favorite part was always Q&A. I realized that we indeed were waking leaders up to a new generation and it comforted me to see so many interested. Considering we always have to stop our speech with so many more hands still in the air, I knew that leaders had a lot of questions. This sparked a research idea of my own. I wanted to ask CEOs to submit one question they want to have answered about Gen Z by Gen Z. My dad said that if I got submissions, we could partner with the Institute for Corporate Productivity to field the survey. Since my dad gave me the green light to run with the survey, I added in celebrities, too.

My goal was to get twenty-five questions and in the end I got forty-four, including from Mark Cuban, Arianna Huffington, and Oprah, to name a few! Throughout the book you will see their questions and survey results.

While most of the people I reached out to got back to me, I still experienced some resistance. Like my dad said, there is some Millennial fatigue out there, which does not bode well for my generation. We've barely showed up at work and some people are already over us? That doesn't seem fair. It also doesn't seem smart. There are 72 million of us. Ignoring Gen Z would be like pretending the entire population of Germany doesn't exist. *Fast Company* reports that by 2020, Gen Z is predicted to make up 40 percent of the population.

However, I get it. You finally think you have it all figured out and then a new generation shows up. It feels like you have to do all the work. Hopefully, by learning about Gen Z earlier on, it won't have to feel like work at all. And if it makes you feel any better, as committed as I am to spreading the word about Gen Z, I'm just as committed to letting my generation know how much we can learn from the other generations.

And no, I'm not just saying that so you will keep reading, but I hope you will.

So to answer your first question . . . why the name Gen Z?

Turn the page and keep reading.

THE NAME GAME

75 Million	Traditionalists Pre 1946
80 Million	Baby Boomers 1946–1964
60 Million	Generation X 1965–1979
82 Million	Millennials 1980–1994
72 Million	Generation Z 1995–2012

Dad, why is it after every speech that one of the first questions I get asked is about the name Gen Z?

Jonah, for as long as I can remember people have been asking me after speeches what the next generation would be called.

What did you say?

Since you were only in diapers, I said I didn't know yet. But now that the leading edge of your group are graduating college you are on the radar and people need to know what to call you.

They seem so surprised that we are okay with the name Gen Z.

Well, for previous generations it's been a hot topic.

Why? It's just a name.

For starters, as authors of this book and speakers/experts on the topic, we are putting our stake in the ground and committing to the name Gen Z for reasons we will explain.

Since I have been asked for more than twenty years what the next generation after the Millennials was going to be called, putting a stake in the ground was not something done lightly. We were anxious to see in our national survey if the name was okay with Gen Zers themselves.

In our national survey, 77 percent of Gen Z respondents said they didn't care or liked the name Gen Z. In every focus group or discussion I have with fellow Gen Zers, no matter how many names I put in front of them, they all gravitate to Gen Z and agree with our rationale.

But first . . .

What's in a Name?

When it comes to the generations, a lot! Especially for marketers who have always liked segmentation as a way to target consumers. When you can understand a group of people better, you can create more appealing messages that will resonate.

Just as marketers have targeted women, men, teens, minority groups, and more . . . generations have proven to be profitable targets. So if you are going to target a group of people, it only seems natural that they would need a name. What marketers really have liked is when a name can just roll off the tongue.

Over the years, generational segmentation has carried over to the workplace. Just as generational preferences have helped marketers to sell, they have also helped employers to hire and manage. It can be useful to have a common language to refer to each other. In fact, generations is the easiest of segments to talk about since there isn't as much political correctness. For example, most employers would tread lightly making a comment like, "We should hire more Asians . . ." but would have no problem saying, "We need to figure out how to recruit more Millennials."

Again, having a name has helped.

The Evolution of Names

So when did the whole naming of a generation begin? Many would think that it started with the oldest living generation and worked its way down. In actuality, the name game began with the Baby Boomers. It all started when the Census Bureau referred to the years between 1946 and 1964 as the Baby Boom, when birthrates went up from approximately 3 million a year to over 4 million a year. As the members of this generation became adults and thus consumers, marketers found great success in marketing their products and services to the so-called Baby Boomers. When it came to the name, Boomers never seemed to balk at it and indeed wore it with a badge of honor. When a generation is garnering the limelight in every market it touches, it feels good to be part of the boom. Even today, as Pew Research reports, 79 percent of Boomers identify with the name and you really don't hear much complaining about it or, for that matter, any alternatives.

And thus, the concept of naming a generation was proven to be worth it or just downright profitable. The Baby Boomers would be the first and last time (to date) a generation's "official" name would come from a government organization.

Generations that came before the Boomers were immediately named retroactively. After all, they were still active consumers, and since grouping the Boomers together was profitable, it would surely be so for the other generations. For a while the generation right before the Boomers was labeled the "Silent Generation," based on the notion that when it came to communication, they were often silent. Boomers accused them of not expressing deep feelings, speaking up at work, or sharing personal information. The problem was that "silent" suggested invisible, and for the generation that beat back the Great Depression, won two world wars, and put a man on the moon, the name really didn't seem to fit.

In the 1990s, my business partner Lynne and I, and many others, went with the term *Traditionalists*. It was originally coined in a *Time* magazine article in 1951, but didn't really get noticed for forty years. The feeling was that they upheld so many traditional values to be proud of that the name seemed more fitting and, let's face it, definitely rolled off the tongue easier. Whenever we asked Traditionalists about the name they typically shrugged their shoulders or ironically were just silent.

In 1998, Baby Boomer and famous TV journalist Tom Brokaw penned the book *The Greatest Generation,* which was about the generation that came before the Traditionalists. Something to note is that the distinction between the Greatest Generation and Traditionalists isn't often made because the two generations are so similar. The two names definitely resonated with everyone and there has never really been another strong contender.

Naming a generation based on a literary work wasn't a new thing. It had happened before Brokaw came out with *The Greatest Generation.* In fact, it was the name of a book that gave birth to the name of the generation that followed the Boomers.

In 1991, Douglas Coupland wrote his book *Generation X: Tales for an Accelerated Culture.* The book described the post-Boomer generation based on the anonymity the author and his contemporaries felt growing up in the shadow of the Baby Boomers. Why "X"? In math *x* is a variable and for a generation feeling lost, the symbolism seemed appropriate.

The problem was that it set a very dim and grim picture of the generation. Rather than be worn as a badge of honor, it was more of a negative label and for many an insult. There was definitely some backlash. However, it did roll off the tongue and made marketers' job all the easier.

As much as Xers didn't like the negative connotation, they were still a generation that was built on a more antiestablishment sentiment and agreed with the culture Coupland was describing. While not as high of a percentage as Boomers, Pew Research reports that today 58 percent of Gen X still identify with the name. In addition, as marketers assessed, the name not only rolls off the tongue, but does sound cool. There have never been any alternatives or even a close second.

When it came time to name the next generation after the Xers, there was a lot of buzz. First of all, these were the children of the Boomers. They were not going to let a negative name ensue, as had happened with Gen X. Second, there were a lot of them, so marketers were especially anxious as they geared up for this next great cash cow.

The first name to appear on the scene was Gen Y. However, whether it was a lack of marketing cachet or solid description, it didn't seem to stick. Once again, it took a book to put a new name out there. Authors and historians Neil Howe and William Strauss coined the term *Millennials* in their 2000 book, *Millennials Rising.* Those of us generational experts, as well as marketers, felt it rolled off the tongue and therefore right into the history books.

It's not that Gen Y totally died, though. In fact, we often have to explain to audiences that Gen Y and Millennials are the same generation. While the name Millennials has stuck for years with marketers and employers, it has struggled lately with the generation itself. Pew reports that only 40 percent of Millennials identified with the name.

In recent years, the Millennials have often been accused by the media of being self-absorbed or entitled. Maybe it's no surprise that they want to distance themselves from the name. Realistically, however, it is too late for a new name to emerge. Just ask the Xers.

So what have we learned?

Gen Z: It Should Be a Name, Not a Label

We can agree that marketers and employers have benefited by targeting generational cohorts and that each one needs a name. However, the conversation has gone south or caused friction when the name tries to describe a given generation.

The Silent Generation didn't like the suggestion of being labeled as invisible. Xers have never gravitated to the idea of being a lost variable, and Millennials who wanted a more descriptive name now seem to want a different one.

So here we are again and a new generation is showing up and already there are a lot of names being thrown out there. It's not just marketers who are interested. We all are looking for a way to talk about generational differences at home and at work. To name more than a few that have been put on the table: 9/11 Generation, Digital Natives, Selfies, Centennials, or iGeneration.

We're going with Gen Z and here's why.

In our national survey, none of the other names resonated at all. Why? No one in my generation wants to be labeled. The reason 77 percent of Gen Z respondents said they didn't care or liked the name Gen Z is that they didn't feel labeled. Instead, it was just a name that symbolizes where we lie on the generational timeline. There are now five living generations. With too many names floating out there, we run the risk of polluting and even worse confusing the generational dialogue. "Gen Z" actually makes it easy. Funny thing is, whenever you read the other suggested names, they all seem to be followed by (Gen Z). So why not just call us that?

It's simple. There was X, then Y, and now Z.

The deeper argument for the name Gen Z is that if any generation won't land on a label, it's our generation. Gen Z is embracing individuality more than ever. Each member of Gen Z is looking to create our own individual brand and stand out. We are the most diverse generation in history, already balking at being labeled by race, gender, religion, and so on—why would a generation label be any different?

However, we totally understand that as marketers try to strategize how to sell to us and employers figure out how to recruit and manage us, we still need a name. As my dad always says, going without a name didn't work for the musician Prince, and it won't work for my generation.

If in time a new name comes out that my generation likes . . . great! However, we doubt it and are going with the name, not the label, Gen Z. It definitely rolls off the tongue and just as most of the other generations that followed the Boomers got their name, it's now in a book!

MOM AND DAD

Hey buddy! How did it go?

Pretty good. I hit a double, struck out, and then got walked.

Not bad.

Check this out.

What is it?

We got a trophy.

You guys won?

No. My coach said it's a participation award.

Jonah, let's be clear. If anyone deserves a trophy, it's me. I got you here on time for the last ten weeks.

There are numerous and different events and conditions that shape a generation. As these events and conditions play out in the lives of each of the generations, they shape the attitudes, values, and work styles that the generations bring with them when they come to work every day. Too many employers and employees don't notice these differences because they assume that since we all experience the same life stages, we must see them all the same way. Don't we all have to be born, be educated, find work, find partners, create families, age, retire, and eventually die? And don't we perform these functions pretty similarly?

The answer is yes, and no. Yes, we all have certain life stages in common, but no, the different generations do not approach them the same way.

Understanding what shapes a generation gives you more insights into the lens each generation is looking through and how they approach different life stages, especially work and career.

We will dive into most of the events and conditions in the next chapter. However, we wanted to start with the one influence that all of the generations share that is definitely the most powerful . . . mom and dad. All of the generations are shaped by those who have raised them.

If anyone is curious whether Gen Z is different from the Millennials, take a step back and think about how different their parents are! For most, Boomers raised Millennials and Gen X raised Gen Z.

For years the differences between Baby Boomers and Gen Xers have not only intrigued the workplace, but also in many ways haunted it. If there is one thing that everyone can agree upon, it's that from communication styles to career aspirations and more, the two generations could not seem further apart. With this in mind, one can only imagine how different their offspring would be.

The Parent Pendulum

If we look at how the generations have parented, there is a pattern. A generation will react to how the one before them did it or how they were raised themselves. They will adopt some "best practices" but will of course believe there is a better way.

Starting with the Boomers . . . Ask most Baby Boomers about their parenting style and it was a lot different from how they were raised themselves. Boomers' parents grew up in a nation of immigrants who wanted to conform or fit in. Where today, for example, having an accent can be cool or even exotic, for Boomers' parents it was not cool. The goal was to do whatever they could to look and sound like an American. Boomers grew up in households that were very strict. Their parents had strong beliefs in what was right or wrong and quoted our forefathers on how to be a good citizen and live an American life.

Roles were crystal clear. Men brought home the bacon, and women cooked it. Basically, the household had structure with a lot of rules and very little, if any, room for leeway. In Boomers' parents' minds, if you followed the rules of civilization you could be very successful. The goal was to be productive, obedient, and respectful. Rules were rules. Their parents told them they could do great things and did what they could to hand their Boomer kids the American dream.

Boomers experienced the growth of the middle class. In addition, the GI Bill opened up opportunities to go to college. They saw firsthand that there were more options than a future in manual labor.

As Boomers spread their wings, as much as they saw more of the world, they also saw a lot that they wanted to change about it. The problem was that they couldn't exactly go to their parents with these ideas. The rules for kids were clear. They were based on a proverb that dates back to the fifteenth century: "Children should be seen, and not heard."

When there was communication with Boomer children, there was not a lot of touchy-feely conversations. It felt militaristic, like a drill sergeant. There was definitely a list of topics that were taboo. Boomers could not have real deep conversations about money, sex, politics, or religion with their parents. Everything felt very black-and-white.

Boomers started to find some gray. In fact, a lot of gray. This was hard to deal with when you felt like you were living in a dictatorship. Boomers didn't feel that their feelings or thoughts were being heard by their parents.

They started to listen to new music and suddenly Thomas Jefferson wasn't the one to quote. Rather it was the Beatles, Grateful Dead, or Bob Dylan.

Boomers really expanded their points of view with the onset of the drug culture, which could unpin their minds from a rigid way of looking at the world.

Boomers also experienced one of the biggest inventions of all time, the television. In 1952, *four* million television sets could be found in American homes. By 1960, the number was *fifty* million! Boomers had a host of new influential people, including Martin Luther King Jr., Abbie Hoffman, John F. Kennedy, Rosa Parks, and Gloria Steinem, all opening minds to a new way the world could and should operate. Suddenly the generation gap widened as an entire generation of Boomers who grew up with television could relate to a whole new set of reference points. And as they fine-tuned their sets, Boomers honed their generational personalities. As much as Boomers wanted to support the institutions that the previous generations had created, they were rocked by tragedies that encouraged them to challenge everything they knew about the respectability of the status quo. They were permanently changed by deep, divisive issues like the war in Vietnam, Watergate, protest and human rights movements, free love, flower power and black power, the women's movement, the OPEC oil embargo, stagflation, and the recession.

Eighteen was the magic age, since it meant you were an "adult" and could move out of the house. Let's be clear: Boomers' parents weren't exactly holding them back and were often the first to open the door and carry their cardboard box out for them.

This generation truly rebelled and it was an era of civil rights, human rights, and voter's rights. As for who should bring home the bacon? Boomer women were not going to settle for black and white. Boomers' rebellion against the structure they grew up in carried right on into how they were going to operate when they became parents themselves.

Boomers: The Groovy Parents

When Boomers started to become moms and dads, their rebellion against how they were raised resulted in a much less rigid and more permissive parenting style. The pendulum was definitely going to swing back.

They wanted to be young, hip, and groovy. They didn't want to turn into rigid old dictators, like they viewed their parents.

The timeline of Boomers becoming parents also paralleled the pop psychology movement. Boomers did not want their Millennial kids to grow up and see the world so black-and-white. The goal was to find your own identity and not feel like a robot. There was a lot of room for gray. In fact, it wasn't gray at all. It was colorful. Every child was like a snowflake—truly one of a kind. Where Boomers grew up with stringent bedtimes or dress codes, Millennials had a lot more flexibility.

With 80 million peers, Boomers have always been competing to stand out from the crowd. When it was time to be parents, this competitive drive only went up a notch. After all, they felt that their Millennial kids were a true reflection of their own success.

Boomers were going to be sure their "snowflakes" were the best they could be and so they were very hands-on. So much so that their parenting style earned them the label of helicopter parents. From sports to language immersion to playing an instrument to volunteering and more . . . if there was a free minute to be had, Boomers made sure their Millennial kids made use of it.

As hard as competitive Boomers worked to have their kids stand out from the crowd, they worked even harder to stand out themselves at the office. And it took a lot of work. It was the beginning of the fight to get ahead.

For Boomers, the time to get to the office was always ten minutes before the boss and you would never leave the office until after your boss. Boomer women especially were fighting hard for a place at the conference table, which made it all the more stressful to find time to be around the dinner table.

Boomers didn't get to see their kids as much as they wanted to and definitely had guilt around this. Boomers focused more on quality time versus quantity of time. If you got home at 6:30 p.m. and bedtime was just a few hours later, the last thing you were going to do during that period was fight with your child. The focus was on praising, not punishing. Rather than yell at their kids to be a certain way, as had happened to them when they were growing up, Boomers instilled a lot of self-esteem into their Millennial kids.

A great gift that Boomers gave their children was opening up the lines of communication like never before. Ask any Millennial about their Boomer parent and they will tell you that communication was anything but militaristic. No topic was taboo when it came to dinnertime conversations.

Boomers believed that their kids should be seen *and* heard.

Boomers are the generation that has always equated work with self-fulfillment. As they did work harder and harder, they achieved the American dream that had been laid out for them. They had big careers, a family, and a house in the suburbs with a white picket fence. Rather than feel as though they had arrived, however, many looked around and wondered, "Is this it?" They struggled since they had given up so much to "make it" and wondered if it was even worth it. As a result, more than just talk to their kids about money, sex, politics, or religion, they talked to their kids about finding what makes them happy in life.

Parents told their Millennial kids that if they were going to have to work as hard as they had, then they should just be sure they were doing something that they really cared about. Don't forget that that was always coupled with a dose of the self-esteem movement, where Millennials were reminded that whatever their decision was, they were going to be great at it. While in many cases that hasn't panned out for Millennials yet, it would be hard to criticize the Boomers for raising children to always try.

It is no wonder that Millennials have turned out to be so communicative and collaborative as well as optimistic and idealistic. On top of that, with Boomer parents pushing their kids to do what makes them the most happy, Millennials naturally are very focused on finding meaning in all that they do.

Probably the biggest nod to Boomer parents is the bond they have been able to create with their kids. Bravo! For the first time in history, when kids were asked who their heroes were, Millennials said "Mom and Dad." It's also the first time that the word *friend* was used to describe a parent.

That's a far cry from how Boomers viewed their own folks. Remember, for them the magic age was eighteen, since it was the golden opportunity to fly the nest. Their parents were right there to open the door and kick them out. Now that Boomers themselves are parents, they too are opening the door, only they are inviting their Millennial kids back in. In fact, Pew Research found that 26 percent of Millennials are living at home with their parents.

Talk about a pendulum swing!

Growing Up X

Unlike the Boomers, Xers didn't grow up with parents who were so focused on drilling rigid structures into them. In fact, Xers craved any parenting at all. Gen X spent less time with mom and dad than previous generations of kids. Gen X was the first generation of latchkey kids, coming home from school to an empty house. They planned their own schedules and made their own meals. Gen Xers keenly remember heading out after school on their bikes, without helmets, and their parents having no clue where they were.

More than just adapting to two working parents, Gen Xers had to adapt to two separate homes. In the 1990s, author Karen Ritchie found that during the birth years of Gen X, the U.S. divorce rate tripled. Single-parent and blended families helped Xers understand that families come in all shapes and sizes and that not everyone lives in a perfect suburban house surrounded by a white picket fence.

They had a new kind of babysitter, one that wasn't even human. Xers' childhood was the era of emerging technology. Much of their time alone could be passed watching cable television. No longer were there just a handful of stations to choose from. Xers had MTV, CNN, ESPN, and so many more. If something didn't catch your eye on TV, you could always plug in Pong, Atari, or Intellivision and play games until mom and dad got home. It was too early for email or social networking with others, since personal computers hadn't quite hit the scene. So these weren't games that Xers played across the network with tons of other kids. They were solo games.

In a nutshell, Xers found themselves home alone and taking care of themselves, and even their siblings, a lot.

Karen Ritchie also found that by the age of twenty, the average Gen Xer had watched 23,000 hours of television. It was the 1980s, when suddenly there was more than the few network stations to watch. Cable television was widespread and there were dozens of channels. Additionally, programming didn't end at midnight with the national anthem followed by

---

ARIANNA HUFFINGTON

Author and Cofounder of the *Huffington Post*

How does Gen Z define success?

TOP RESPONSE: Have a loving, healthy family

What's the most important thing Gen Z wants in a workplace?

TOP RESPONSE: Respect

---

a blank screen. Programming didn't end at all; it was on all day and all night. Part of what this "babysitter" did was expose Xers to different cultures right in their own home dens. At the same time, it also painted a bleak future for Gen X. Xers watched a lot of political and institutional incompetence. All the institutions that Baby Boomers had fought so hard to change, Xers watched being called into question. I'll never forget in one of my earliest focus groups an Xer said, "You name the institution, I'll name the crime."

During their teen years of the 1980s, the economy took a nosedive and, for the first time in history, we had a generation that was told that they would not do as well as their parents or the Boomers.

Suddenly, the American dream had changed. It wasn't even about "making it"; it was about "surviving it."

Xers' childhoods resulted in an independent and survival mentality that was loaded with a healthy dose of skepticism. They had just seen too many leaders and institutions be built up and then fall down.

As they grew older, this mentality carried right into how they were going to operate when they became parents themselves.

Gen Xers: The Nesting Parents

Just as we learned a lot about Millennials by understanding how they were raised, looking at the Xer parent will shed a lot of light as we now turn our attention to Gen Z.

When Xers started having kids, they wanted to create the

homes that they didn't have growing up. For starters, Xers were going to do everything possible not to end up divorced. Xers got married later in life. Where the average marrying age in 1950 was 23 for men and 20 for women, in 2009 it was 28 for men and 26 for women. They wanted to be sure. The good news is that divorce rates are now at their lowest since 1970.

Xers were also going to be sure to be around more and not leave their Gen Z kids home alone as much as they had been. It was an era of nesting that gave birth to experts like Martha Stewart, who could show you how to do it all, from turning a pumpkin into a soup bowl to making a runner out of old mittens. According to Harvard's Joint Center for Housing Studies, Xers' push for the perfect nest also pushed them to take out more home equity loans and spend more on remodeling, per capita, than previous generations.

Gen X parents threw Boomers' main focus on quality time out the window. They felt it was a cop-out and that quantity is equally as important. They were not willing to sacrifice their time at home for that next promotion at the office. They didn't have to, either. Because they were smaller in number than the Boomers, they didn't feel the same competitive pressures. Sure, they wanted to do well, but they weren't paying the same price for success. They triggered the hard push for work-life balance in the workplace.

Where Boomers remember a television commercial for an AT&T product that pitched helping you get more done at the office, Xers saw commercials that pitched the same technology being used to help you stay more connected to home.

Having witnessed the repercussions of two working parents, as well as calculating that the costs of day care were often a wash, many Xer couples chose to have one parent stay at home. Unlike previous generations, it was not black-and-white who was bringing home the bacon.

For my generation, having a dad at home or even around was more common. One in seven stay-at-home parents today is a dad, compared to one in one hundred in 1970. Bottom line was that for Gen Z, we were told that it didn't matter who was the breadwinner, just as long as there was bread.

One of my first memories of my dad being on TV was when he was on the *Today* show around Father's Day. The story was all about how Gen X men were changing diapers, cooking dinner, and raising kids while the moms went off to work. Seems weird that that was newsworthy.

Where Boomer women remember fighting so hard to be respected in the office, many Gen X men recall fighting to be respected in the roles they could play at home. I remember interviewing a lot of stay-at-home dads who would talk about being left out of conversations in the school pickup lines or not asked to be classroom helpers. They were offended by how, in the media, men would be portrayed as bumbling idiots who barely knew how to cook something in the microwave, let alone do a load of laundry.

My generation has seen gender roles redefined. In addition, more than just highly involved dads, we have seen the definition of a nuclear family evolve as well. Like our Gen X parents learned, families could come in all shapes and sizes. For Gen Z, we have

RACHEL THOMAS
President and Cofounder of LeanIn.org

Do you think your generation sees women and men differently than your parents' generation did?

Yes: 90 percent
No: 10 percent

For those who answered "yes," what do you think has changed?

TOP 3 RESPONSES
Feminist movement
More equality in all facets of life
Gender roles have disappeared

grown up where a family can have two moms or two dads. It may not be the majority, but one thing is for sure: it isn't surprising or a big deal at all.

Regardless of what the family looks like or what roles are being played . . . the biggest message that has been loud and clear to my generation is that family comes first.

In school, there have been a lot of initiatives to encourage us to create family mealtimes. In elementary school, I remember a big push for family game nights. I feel so lucky because my family eats together at least four nights a week. We have been very committed to family meals, even waiting to eat until I get home from snowboarding practice as late as eight o'clock. As youth, many of us have probably taken this for granted, but as we now are older and launching careers of our own, we will not only appreciate the family time that our Gen X parents fought for, but also want to keep on fighting ourselves. The battle between work and life is only going to get more intense as we get jobs and have to balance them with our personal lives and families.

Riding the High-Tech Helicopter

Jonah, I thought you said you were going to a movie.

I am.

Then why do I see on my phone that your car is parked at Josie's house?

We met there and then all went in Miles's car.

Got it.

As notorious as Baby Boomers became for their "helicopter" parenting style, Gen X has taken it to a whole new level. However, it's hard to know if Gen Xers are hovering more than Boomers because they want to, because it's just become that much easier, or because it is more commonly expected.

Technology has changed the parenting game. Today, there are more apps and tools than ever before to know where your kids are and what they are doing at all times.

Beyond just providing the joys of GPS, technology at your fingertips has also changed the parenting game by opening up a library of resources and advice. This has taken protectiveness to a whole new level. With access to an army of mommy bloggers, Gen X parents have been warned about shielding their Gen Z kids from elements that never used to be an issue. From how you wash a baby bottle to toys being free of BPA to ergonomic strollers to backward-facing infant car seats, you name it! This is quite the pendulum swing. Xers are parenting a lot differently than how they were raised. They would never imagine letting their Gen Z kids head out the door on their bikes (especially without a helmet) all day and have no clue of their whereabouts.

Still Heroes and Friends

As we saw the Boomers do so well with their Millennial kids, Xers wanted to create a special bond with their Gen Z kids. Xers can be just as proud that their children see them as heroes and friends as well. In fact, according to a study done by Nickelodeon, two-thirds of Gen X parents say they're closer to their children than they were to their parents. Eighty-three percent of Gen Xers consider their children to be their best friends.

Again, technology has played a large role. For Boomers and Millennials, technology was more of a divide. Millennials had to help their Boomer parents do everything from download a ringtone to learn how to text. The ramp-up was hard for Boomers and caused a lot of gaps. Xers, on the other hand, are just as comfortable with technology as their Gen Z kids. The result has been that there are now more similarities than ever before in history between parents and children, ranging from tastes in music and clothes to the activities they engage in. However, just because Xers have an easier time logging on, it doesn't mean they are always in the know. Like all kids, Gen

Z is quick to figure out ways to hide things from their parents. Gen Xers still have to work hard at keeping up and tuned in to all that their Gen Z kids are doing.

Jonah! I can't believe you are wearing my dress shirt!

Did Mom tell you?

No . . . I just saw your post on Snapchat and clearly you're wearing my shirt!

So busted.

Yup! I've told you a million times that you have to ask me before going into my closet.

Dang!

Gone are the days where you fight with your parents for singing the lyrics to "Lucy in the Sky with Diamonds" or for swinging your hips to Elvis's "Jailhouse Rock."

My generation jams with our parents to everyone from Drake to Taylor Swift to Michael Jackson. My dad asks me all the time who I'm listening to. Not because he wants me to turn it off, but more because he wants to download it for his own playlist.

Perhaps even more significant than Xers' bond with their Gen Z kids over fashion, music, activities, and more is Gen Z's influence over their parents' wallet. According to the Nickelodeon study, more than ever before, kids are influencing family purchasing decisions. For example, 71 percent of parents solicit and consider their kids' opinions when making purchases; 95 percent of parents seek their kids' opinions when buying products for themselves.

JEFF WEINER
CEO of LinkedIn

Twenty to thirty years from now, looking back at your career, what would you like to say you accomplished?

TOP RESPONSE: I was able to give my family a good life.
CLOSE SECOND: I made a difference in the world.

We aren't always talking about what kind of potato chips to buy or color of lipstick. In a different study by JWT Intelligence, 65 percent of moms said Gen Z influences the purchasing of vacations, 32 percent said home furnishings, and 29 percent said cars. These are big purchases.

Just like we saw with the Millennials when they came to work, Gen Z will assume they should be consulted on big decisions in the workplace. If you're helping your parents plan a vacation or buy a house, it will only seem natural that you weigh in on whether to acquire a new business or piece of office equipment.

It is understandable that managers might be nervous about the impact of the tight bond between Gen X parents and their Gen Z kids. After all, the close parent-child dynamic has been a problem since Millennials showed up at work. For Millennials it felt normal to see their boss as a potential friend. They often put managers in awkward situations, ranging from whether to accept a friend request on Facebook to whether they should attend the happy hour. Never mind managers just having to navigate friendships with the new Millennial recruit; many were taken for a loop when they heard from their employees' Boomer parents as well. Managers were definitely caught off guard when Boomer parents did everything from show up at orientation to call the boss to complain about their child's review.

However, as close as Gen X parents are with their Gen Z kids, managers won't have to worry as much.

For starters, probably the biggest warning our Xer parents instilled in us is to be careful with technology and communication. Unlike the Boomers, our parents definitely knew all the ins and outs. It was drilled into our heads that we need to think through every friend request and post. Our Xer parents have had plenty of examples to share where someone put something online that should have been kept offline. We will want to get along with our bosses, but we won't be as quick to cross the line when it comes to sharing too much information or being friends.

As for bosses getting a phone call from Gen Z's mom and dad? Not as likely. Harking back a bit to how they were raised themselves, Xers will be more hands-off. Sure, Xers have always wanted to be there to support their Gen Z kids, but they are taking a big step back when it comes to rescuing them. One of Xers' proudest parenting traits has been to let their kids fail, as they feel some of your best life lessons will come from it. If something doesn't go so well on the job, it will be Gen Z's job to fix it. They may consult their parents, but they wouldn't dream of their parents stepping in and doing the dirty work. Besides, Xers made way too much fun of the Boomers for calling the boss on behalf of their Millennial kids to even consider doing it themselves.

It's a Tough World Out There

Hey Jonah, I just read your parts for the "Phigital" chapter.

What did you think?

It's not good and definitely needs to be rewritten. You need to explain yourself better.

Wow . . . Not even a "good try, Jonah"?

No. Do you think that's what a book critic would say?

I'll redo it.

Gen X has raised their Gen Z kids with a very direct and unfiltered communication style. Xers have never beat around the bush when it comes to telling their kids what they think. It could be feedback on a school paper or their plans for the future. If Xers think it isn't good, they say so and don't waste time padding the message. Where Boomers told their kids that the sky is the limit, Xers told Gen Z that the sky is often falling. Remember, Xers were told that they would do worse than the previous generations. Also, they grew up during a lot of economic distress in the 1980s.

More than hearing our parents tell stories of the past, Gen Z has grown up witnessing it firsthand ourselves. Our formative years saw the worst recession in decades. Gen Z watched parents lose jobs. We witnessed companies and industries crumble. It didn't take a lot of convincing for us that indeed it was a tough world out there.

Xers felt that the right thing to do was to prepare their kids for the real world. It started with the most basic lesson of all: In life, there are winners and there are losers. Xers don't believe in the Boomer parenting philosophy that if everyone works hard together, we can all win. Xers are going to be sure that their Gen Z kids know how to lose just as well as win. Like all parents, Xers encourage the importance of putting in your best effort; however, they don't believe that you should be rewarded just for trying.

Has all of the Xers' straight talk gone too far? We heard from a lot of teachers who felt Gen Z was very serious and at times too serious. We heard comments like "They seem so worried about issues that most kids don't think about" or "They are so focused on tomorrow that they don't seem to be able to live for today." Most adults long for the days where they weren't concerned about mortgages, next career moves, paying bills, etc. They keenly remember the days of just being carefree kids. Xers' push to prepare them for the real world has the risk of Gen Z not enjoying the days of just being kids. When Gen Z shows up at work, will they be like their skeptical parents, who are always preparing for the worst of times? This didn't bode well for Xers, who were labeled as the resident downers. It's one thing to be real and even ready for the future; it's another if Gen Z becomes constantly fearful of what's ahead and doesn't learn to live for and even enjoy being in the moment.

The Road Less Traveled

Xer parents witnessed other generations fail to get to where they wanted to go. Gen Xers were skeptical of most traditional institutions and felt they needed to figure out their own independent way.

Of course this played out when it came to parenting. Take the institution of education. Rather than work with many of the public institutions, Gen X simply took matters into their own hands—literally. The U.S. Department of Education reports that between 2003 and 2012, the number of American children between ages 5 to 17 who were homeschooled rose 62 percent. From 1999 to 2013, the percentage of charter schools increased from 1.7 to 6.2 percent.

Xers also watched pioneering Boomers like Bill Gates and Steve Jobs break away and work alone in a garage to start their own gig. As the famous Apple slogan from the 1990s goes, they felt free to "think different." Xers felt this independence wasn't something to be shunned, but rather emulated since it could actually become lucrative.

So rather than tell their kids to fall in line, Xers told Gen Z to make their own line.

We were told that we don't have to follow the traditional paths of education and careers. We were encouraged to expose ourselves to as many different opportunities as possible and to always draw our own conclusions—even if they weren't popular. The message was loud and clear that you didn't have to worry about what everyone else was doing and that it was okay, even cool, to find your own way.

In the next chapter we dive deeper into the events and conditions that have shaped Gen Z. However, getting your arms around how they were parented is a great start to understand where Gen Z is coming from and why they will think and act like they do.

We can be ready for a more realistic, straight-shooting, competitive, and independent bunch.

What's even crazier is that we can start to get a snapshot of the generation that comes *after* Gen Z. Thankfully, they won't be hitting the workplace for a while and we don't have to do anything . . . but if you want to even start thinking about them, then take a peek at the parents who will be raising them.

Millennials Are No Longer the Kids . . . They're Having Them!

That's right! Millennials are becoming parents. According to *Time* magazine, 47 percent are already moms and dads. While it's always fun for those who have been through it already to watch the newest generation take the stroller for a spin, it can definitely be strategic to keep an eye on this next generation. As for what we will call them . . . that's for a different book.

If we look at how Millennials are parenting, it is clear that their bond with their Boomer parents is playing out. Many of the trends that they experienced as kids are actually ones that they want to uphold now that they are mom and dad. If anything, they want to take it up a notch. For example, we all know about Boomers' infamous focus on instilling self-esteem. Millennials are determined to keep the self-esteem movement going strong. They will be sure their kids all feel like one-of-a-kind snowflakes. In fact, they see their kids as so unique that they may even name them "Snowflake." *Time* reported that 60 percent of Millennial parents believe it is somewhat, very, or extremely important that their child's name be unique.

Similar to their Baby Boomers parents, Millennials are creating familial mini democracies where everyone has a voice and vote. The fifteenth-century proverb that "children should be seen, and not heard" is still dead. Just as Baby Boomer parents encouraged their children to speak up, so too do Millennials now that they have children. We can only imagine the level of collaboration that they will achieve.

Although Millennials mimic their parents in many ways, they are still developing their own unique parenting styles.

Boomers got advice from the one and only expert, Dr. Spock. Along came Xers, who, as we mentioned, could tap into countless mommy bloggers offering up tips and advice. Millennials have been consistently tribal. Therefore, they rely heavily on the collective opinions of their peers in order to make decisions. They witnessed the transition from Web-based experts to peer reviews and discussions. From the best stroller to pick to what preschool to attend to even how best to navigate a trip to Disney, Millennials are connected to one another and constantly seeking advice and recommendations from each other. And even if you aren't looking for advice, Millennials aren't shy to share it. Their collaborative nature combined with social media has resulted in a 24/7 highlight reel of their lives.

What parent hasn't wanted to brag about their children? Millennial parents were given a megaphone with social media. It's fine if you want to see what high chair to buy, but it can also have a negative impact as parents watching these reels can't help but compare themselves. The problem is that the majority of the time, the only reel you see is the one with "happily ever after." Everyone will post the picture of their kid at breakfast hugging Mickey. But how many post a picture ten hours later when the same kid is coming down from a sugar high and didn't have a nap?

The perfect moments are advertised and the reality is hidden. This can leave Millennial parents feeling insecure and anxious about their own abilities as a parent. In a *Time* survey of 2,700 U.S. mothers, they found that 80 percent of Millennial moms said it's important to be "the perfect mom." This could be one of the reasons that there are more Millennial stay-at-home parents than any other generation.

As the competition for best parent heats up, more Millennial parents are opting to make parenting their full-time job. Could our future workforce after Gen Z take perfectionism to a whole new level? Might they be more inclined to be anxious?

One big difference between Baby Boomer and Millennial parenting involves "playdate culture." As mentioned, Baby Boomers made sure that every second counted and they typically had each day scheduled with various activities. While the intention was good, Millennials who experienced it are pulling back this pendulum.

Millennials now see the dangers of being overscheduled because they see the negative consequences within themselves. Even now, Millennials have difficulty with idle time. Many Millennials are aware of this deficiency and they want their children to learn what to do with "boredom." Millennials are attempting to alleviate the "playdate culture" in exchange for a culture of free time, where children have to find creative ways to entertain themselves.

Might competitive and driven Gen Z managers struggle because at last we have a future workforce after them who will actually know how to chill out a bit? Or will they be thrilled to have a workforce that can structure their time independently rather than constantly checking in?

Another pendulum swing with Millennial parents results from watching how Xers have raised Gen Z. Driving by kids sitting in the backseat with headphones and playing on an iPad has made Millennials think twice about screen time. While they will admit they can be the greatest culprits themselves, they are working hard to instill some "digital detox." As cool as Xers thought it was to give their Gen Z kids a toy that could talk, walk, and blink lights, Millennial parents are stripping away the batteries and opting for more simple and

FREDERICK HUNTSBERRY

Former Chief Operating Officer, Paramount Pictures

Social media allows us to be connected 24/7, but technology can also be isolating. How important are shared live experiences—going out to movie theaters, spending the day at a theme park with family and friends, etc.?

79 percent of Gen Z said it is important or very important.

tangible entertainment. Who would have thought that building blocks would make a comeback? We can only imagine how this will show up at the office someday.

So as fascinating as it might be to look at how Millennials' kids might turn out, for now they are still in diapers. Our bigger task at hand is paying attention to Gen Z, who is not only long out of diapers, but showing up at work. We talked about how parenting has impacted them, let's take a look at Gen Z's other events and conditions and how they shaped who they are today.

EVENTS AND CONDITIONS

Dad. Do you remember where you were when the space shuttle *Challenger* exploded?

Of course. I was in eleventh grade. We had been following the whole journey of the schoolteacher Christa McAuliffe going up in space. I was in Social Studies and we were watching it live on TV. We had party hats on, streamers, and even a cake.

What happened?

Well . . . it took off, and we all cheered. Then suddenly there were clouds of smoke and you didn't know what had happened. It was surreal. I can picture it like it was yesterday. I can even remember what I was wearing that day.

Did people cry?

Actually, I remember there was an eerie silence. Even when

I think about it today, it feels haunting. It changed my generation forever.

Ask a Traditionalist where they were on D-Day, and they will tell you. Ask a Baby Boomer where they were when Kennedy was shot and they too will be able to relive it like yesterday. What Millennial doesn't recall every detail of their whereabouts on 9/11? Every generation has its life-defining moments. Learning about these and the impact they had helps us understand what shapes a generation.

It's very easy to get caught up on using birth years to define a generation. Especially when those of us who have been researching, writing, consulting, and speaking about them all have different ranges. The truth of the matter is that there really isn't a magic age that makes you a member of a generation. It's not as though someone who was born on January 1, 1965, is automatically a Gen Xer and not a Boomer. Birth years are a starting point to help people get their minds wrapped around the different generations. The true learning comes from going beyond birth years.

Ageless Thinking

While generational experts may not all concur on exact birth years, we all do agree that if you really want to understand a generation, you have to go beyond age and look at how each generation shares a common history. The results of these events and conditions lead each generation to adopt its own unique "generational personality." You take a Baby Boomer who watched NASA put a man on the moon and compare that to an Xer who watched the space shuttle *Challenger* explode, and you'll see that attitudes and even behaviors are going to shift.

Events and conditions can include all kinds of things. For example, they can be day-to-day icons like our heroes, sports stars, slogans, favorite products, or songs. Or they can be actual events, such as the Watergate scandal, the civil rights and women's rights movements, wars, or 9/11. Conditions are the forces at work in the environment as each generation comes of age. The Cold War was a condition that permeated the youth of many Boomers, while Millennials born after 1989 will never know a world in which there were two different cities called East and West Berlin.

Too often when two generations bump up against each other, they try to figure out who is right or wrong, better or worse. Those conversations lead nowhere because the truth of the matter is that the generations are just different. Each generation has its own point of view that is valid. Rather than work hard at figuring out who is right or wrong, better or worse, the generations need to try to understand where the others are coming from and why they think the way they do.

We all innately know what shaped our own generation. However, it can be a lot harder to take off your own generational lens and see the world through a different one. But only then can we not only embrace these differences, but bridge the gaps between the generations.

The best way to do this is to look at the events and conditions that shape a generation. It has proven to be successful in bridging so many gaps between Traditionalists, Baby Boomers, Gen Xers, and Millennials.

Like my dad said, you have to take off your own generational lens.

So here is the lens that Gen Z is looking through.

Diversity

As mentioned in "Name Game," Gen Z does not want to be labeled. The biggest reason is that we are too diverse to ever land on one name that could actually describe or label us. In fact, Gen Z is the most diverse generation. The U.S. Census Bureau reports that we have experienced a 50 percent increase in the multiracial youth population since 2000. Gen Z will be the last generation with a white Caucasian majority. The Hispanic teen population is the fastest growing in the United States.

Where it gets tricky is that *diversity* is still such a loaded word. Each generation seems to have its own definition. Sometimes it can even feel weird to talk about it. Gen Z might feel as though we are drawing more attention to something and making it more of an issue than it needs to be. It can feel too obvious to say that we should recognize what makes us all unique. We also don't want to feel as though we are labeling people when it shouldn't matter. Granted, it's probably easier for the white dude to say that . . . but my generation has only known a world where you embrace diversity.

We talk more about it in the chapter on hyper-custom, but for

Gen Z, it's important to know that it goes way beyond race and ethnicity.

Economy

The state of the economy will definitely have an impact on any generation's outlook on the world. For Gen Z, this is one of our biggest influences. Throughout much of middle and high school most of us have heard over and over just how bad the economy is. Our childhood was even being compared and contrasted to the Great Depression. Only ours was being called the Great Recession. Depression or recession—when you're in your teens, it's hard to know what the difference even is. However, one thing is for sure: We knew that it was bad.

In school, we would learn about the Great Depression. I remember one of my social studies assignments was to interview someone who had lived through it or who was raised by parents who did. We all then shared what we learned from these interviews. There was one common theme: Their lives were changed forever by the fear of not having a job or being able to put food on the table.

Then we go home and conversations around our own dinner table felt very similar. We overheard conversations about what companies were closing or whose parents were losing their jobs. A Rutgers University study found that 73 percent of Americans were personally affected by the Great Recession. As we talked about in the "Mom and Dad" chapter, we weren't exactly raised by parents who protected us from the realities of it all.

There is no denying that Millennials' dinner table conversations were much more upbeat and a lot different than ours. Millennials' formative years took place in the mid-1980s through mid-1990s. Millennials heard a lot about stability and opportunity and experienced a killer middle class. They were told to always explore their interests. As we learned about their Boomer parents, throw in some self-esteem on steroids and who wouldn't believe that there were incredible opportunities ahead. In many ways, Millennials could put off thinking about the future and enjoy just being kids.

For Gen Z, we saw the middle class as something that was starting to go away. We have been led to believe that opportunities are a lot tougher to come by and that staying afloat will be a challenge, never mind making the big bucks. As much as we may want to be carefree kids, worries are front and center. In our survey when asked if we were about fun, only 26 percent of Gen Z said yes, compared to double that (52 percent) of Millennials at the same age. We had no choice but to think about the future and if anything was being put off, it was the ability to just be a kid.

My late uncle Howie had a great saying: "You can't fall off the floor." Granted, things can only get better for us as we get older. But when you start on the floor, it definitely instills a fear of falling down again. It's hard not to be scared. It's also hard not to have some tough skin as you gear up to launch your career and try to create a life for yourself.

War on Terrorism

Dad, did you do lockdown drills when you were in high school?

No.

Then how did they train you?

For what?

School shootings.

They didn't have to. There weren't any. The only drills I remember were for fires or tornadoes.

More than the state of the economy, adding to our fears has been the overall state of the world. All the generations have had to deal with unrest. Traditionalists fought in World War II and the Korean War. Boomers of course had Vietnam and Xers came of age during the Gulf War. While each of these wars is very different, one common factor is that they all took place far away.

What started with the Millennials and has continued with my generation is a different war—the war on terrorism. And this war has gotten closer and closer to home. Columbine, Oklahoma City, Virginia Tech, and of course 9/11 have all made it clear as day that no place is safe or sacred anymore. I had the honor of meeting Tom Brokaw, who has written books about the Greatest Generation (Traditionalists). I asked him if he saw similarities between that generation and Gen Z. He reminded me that Traditionalist men as young as eighteen had no choice but to go overseas and fight for their country and that they were the most loyal and patriotic generation ever.

Not as many Gen Zers are climbing into uniform and fighting for our country, and as a whole, we may not be as patriotic. As I've thought about his remarks, in many ways, I wish my generation was told what we could and must do for our country and its safety.

I'm not belittling what the Greatest Generation had to do. I can't

HER MAJESTY QUEEN NOOR

Queen of Jordan and World Activist

How much value would you place on your work connections with people and institutions outside of your country?

55 percent said it's important or very important.
19 percent said it's not important.

imagine how scary it must have been at eighteen to leave home and go fight for your country overseas. However, it's also pretty scary living in a country where you go to school and wonder if someone will show up with a gun. The Greatest Generation could at least feel as though they were banding together to fight. For Gen Z, the only thing we are told we can do is report to someone if we see something suspicious. It's hard not to feel helpless or that things are getting worse. Even horrific acts like suicide bombings, which you used to hear about happening somewhere else, are showing up in our own airports, malls, and stadiums.

Add to that what I'll call modern-day terrorism. These are new attacks that are taking place in our other world, the online one. We are hearing daily about companies like Sony or Target (and so many more) whose computer systems have been hacked and whose customer information is no longer safe. With more and more of our day-to-day lives taking place online, this type of terrorism is only the beginning.

The enemy that we are experiencing isn't a country but a group of extreme radicals who hate us for wanting a life that we have always believed was part of the American dream.

Unlike World War II, or the Korean, Vietnam, or Gulf wars, the reality of our war is that it will never come to an end. It is just something we have come to live with. No, we aren't going to hide or stop living our lives, but safety and security is top of mind. As it should be.

Environment

My dad shared with me that when he was young there was a big push to clean up the planet. He showed me a television commercial from his childhood with a Native American canoeing down a river and becoming emotional from all the littering. It's great that even in the 1970s attention was being put on our environment. But it also seemed too simple to say that all you had to do was stop littering. That feels so obvious. It also doesn't seem clear what the risks were if you didn't stop littering. For Millennials and my generation we have learned that the environment is more than something to keep clean and looking pretty; it is something to protect or beware of. It has always been hammered into our heads that using aerosol spray and Freon creates a hole in the ozone. Even if you weren't exactly clear on what would happen if there was a hole in the ozone, it just sounded scary. The message about littering was more than upsetting Native Americans; it was a crime. We learned to set up composting systems for our families and how to be savvy consumers. We are often the ones to educate our parents on what soap or detergent to buy. In school, there were three new R's that we learned—reduce, reuse, and recycle.

Gen Z joins Millennials in doing all that we can to protect our planet. What is different for Gen Z is that during our formative years, we have seen Mother Nature fight back. There have always been natural disasters, but over the past decade, it seems that they've grown in both scope and frequency. Tsunamis, earthquakes, superstorms, or sinkholes are now common stories on the local news.

Gen Z has grown up in a world where the consequences of our environmental neglect are right outside our windows. We feel the pressure not only to find ways to fix the negative impact we have on the environment, but also to figure out how to live with the consequences of the damage that has already been done.

Politics

Dad, it's amazing how everyone is so quick to accuse my generation of not caring about our right to vote.

Well, if you look at voter turnout, the younger generation has not exercised that right as much as they could or should.

But that doesn't mean we don't care about our right.

What else could it mean?

Maybe it just means that we don't like the candidates or believe our vote will make a difference.

One of my childhood memories was skipping a morning of school to go with my dad to vote in the 2008 election. It was Senator Barack Obama versus Senator John McCain. I was only nine years old. Let's be honest, at that age it was just awesome to get to skip first period. My dad wanted me to come because he said I would always remember the day—and I will.

My dad brought me into the booth with him. It felt very exciting and although I was young, I could still grasp the fact that history was being made as our country elected the first African-American president. While I did have to go to school after he voted, he still let me stay up late to watch the results come in and the announcement being made.

I don't remember what President Obama said after he and his family walked onto the stage to give his acceptance speech. But I do remember all the people they showed around the country crying and celebrating. For a few weeks after, there was a lot of buzz, but then Vikings football season was in full force and, well—like with many nine-year-old boys, that's where my attention went.

The next presidential campaign I truly remember is 2016. Obama's election did prove that the young vote can make a difference and therefore many of the candidates were talking about how their platform connected with the young vote. My dad and I went to the Iowa caucuses to cover the Gen Z vote.

The problem was that no candidate was talking to or about my generation. They all referred to the young voters as Millennials. This was concerning in that politicians have a lot of work to do with my generation. Granted, those Gen Zers (18–21 years old) eligible to vote make up a small segment. However, the Gen Z vote should not have been underestimated especially since it was the first time our generation was able to show up at the polls.

Gen Z voters ages 18–21 add up to a potential 14 million voters.

Considering some of the narrow margins that have gotten presidents into office, that is nothing to ignore. Go beyond just those eligible to vote and there are millions more Gen Zers, like myself, who can go door-to-door or make calls to help a campaign. Yet not one was addressing us specifically.

As we talked with Gen Z voters, we could see they had big concerns that we weren't sure were even on candidates' minds to talk to us about. Of course, candidates put a lot of focus on the cost of education and how they could make college more affordable. At the same time, we heard even more about the cost of health care and how Gen Z is worried about health. This is not something you would typically think is on a young voter's mind. After all, we just assume that the younger you are, the more invincible you feel. However, Gen Z is growing up in a world where, the Centers for Disease Control and Prevention predicts, one in three Americans will have diabetes by 2050. We are worried about the future health of our generation.

We even heard about new issues, such as benefits for freelancers, that politicians weren't talking about with any generation. Yet *Forbes* reports that by 2025, 40 percent of our workforce will be freelance. If politicians are not getting to know about concerns like these and many more, how will they ever know what makes Gen Z unique? How will they be able to connect with us? As I said, they have a lot of work to do.

As my generation has gotten older and now more engaged in politics, I only wish the feelings were more exciting, like what I felt that day in 2008 with my dad at the polling center. Politics have just never been put in a positive light for Gen Z. At least in Millennials' formative years, politics still included collaboration. They did witness politicians reaching across the aisle to get things done.

Even politicians like Senators Ted Kennedy and Orrin Hatch, who could not have been further across the aisle, were friends who often collaborated. They came together to push forward important legislation. My generation has seen nothing but political polarization. I've never known a world where Democrats and Republicans work together.

All I've seen is the two parties actively work to block the other's progress, and any sort of hands reaching across the aisle is a bad thing—even labeled as betrayal. Gen Z does not see Congress as being productive, but rather as vindictive.

It's thus very telling and not surprising that according to a study by Northeastern University, only 3 percent of Gen Z considers politicians to be their foremost role models.

In all of our focus groups and conversations at the Iowa caucuses, it had nothing to do with whether or not we appreciated our right to vote; it was whether or not we truly felt our vote could make a difference. We question if politics is the best vehicle to get things done. Before those who fought for the right to vote judge us, you have to put yourself in our shoes.

It's not as though we think the political process is completely useless and can't get anything done. There is no denying that seeing the legalization of gay marriage or even marijuana during our formative years does instill some hope that progress can be made. What we will need to see more of is government not being all about the politics, and instead focused on the people the politicians were elected to serve.

We can't help but wonder if the best thing to do is work around the system rather than within it.

Celebrity and Media

It's sort of a weird transition from politics to celebrity and media. Then again, when one of the first candidates Gen Z can vote for includes Donald Trump . . . maybe not.

When it comes to events and conditions that shape the generations, there are some things that don't change. Gen Z is influenced by their own list of celebrities from movies, television, music, and sports. Just as Elvis, Michael Jackson, and Michael Jordan rocked the previous generations' worlds, so too are Justin Bieber, Taylor Swift, Kim Kardashian, and LeBron James rocking ours. And while these celebs may not be on posters on our bedroom walls like the Boomers or Xers had, they are all over our screen savers and phone cases.

One big difference when it comes to celebrities with Gen Z is the term *Internet famous.* For every film, TV, or music star today, there is also a YouTube star who came out of nowhere. My generation would argue that these stars are just as famous and influential. A study by *Variety* magazine states that YouTube stars are more popular than mainstream celebs among Gen Z. Sensations such as Kid President, Dude Perfect, and PewDiePie are not just entertaining my generation; they are also sending the message that anyone really can be a star, right from their own bedroom, overnight.

The other difference is that we can get more up close and personal with our icons.

■ ■ ■

Dad! I got a question from Mark Cuban.

You're kidding me.

I'm serious.

How did you do that?

He has his own app called Cyber Dust. I downloaded it and sent him a message. How cool that he replied.

I can't lie, I would have probably called his office and asked for his secretary.

That's why you didn't get the question.

Where Boomers would wait hours just to see one of the Beatles walk off an airplane, Gen Z has Instagram and Twitter feeds that give us personal details down to the minute. Rather than have journalists tell us what's happening in our celebrity icons' lives, we can hear about it directly from the celebrities themselves. Go one step further and we can communicate right back. That's a far cry from Boomers, whose only attempt at being heard by the Beatles depended on who could scream the loudest.

There is no doubt that technology has changed the game when it comes to entertaining my generation. Growing up where bandwidth has never been a limiting factor, we have been able to take entertainment literally into our own hands.

The network and cable TV that Boomers, Xers, and Millennials grew up with feels not only old, but in fact limiting and even boring. Where other generations came home from school and turned on the TV and watched whatever was on, my generation comes home and decides to watch whatever we are in the mood for. We can truly customize our entertainment to exactly what we want. We simply turn on our computer, phones, tablets, and desktops. The Centers for Disease Control and Prevention found that 41 percent of Gen Z spends more than three hours per day on our computers for non-schoolwork-related purposes (compared to 22 percent a decade ago).

Digital platforms such as Netflix, Amazon, Hulu, Apple TV, and YouTube have put a different kind of remote control in our hands. Media for my generation is about being totally mobile and on our terms—what we want, and where and when we want it. Piper Jaffray reported that teens are spending more time on Netflix and YouTube as opposed to traditional TV; the amount of time we spend on these websites combined equates to 59 percent versus traditional TV at 29 percent. The YouTube Generation Study found that among Millennials, YouTube accounts for two-thirds of the premium online video watched across devices. I can only imagine that it is higher for my generation and will continue to soar. YouTube Brandcast explained it well: "We're living in a multi-screen, multi-platform world, where one-in-three consumers say they've never had cable or no longer do. People may be watching less television . . . but they don't love video any less. As TV time goes down, time with online video goes up." It's crazy to think that by 2025, one-half of viewers under the age of thirty-two will not subscribe to a pay TV service.

And even when we do watch traditional TV, it is still on our terms. Think about something like a TV commercial. I can't remember the last time I watched one. I just hit the fast-forward button.

Gen Z is the ultimate consumer of what marketers have called snack media. We like to be entertained in bite sizes. Any YouTube video that is more than two minutes is way too long.

Technology

So clearly technology has opened the door to how my generation has been entertained. However, technology has obviously done a lot more than that for my generation.

In fact, of all the influences on my generation, the one that everyone seems to focus on is technology. I have grown up being plugged in 24/7 with screens everywhere, from riding in backseats of minivans with screens in the headrest in front of me to iPads being handed out in middle school to help me and my peers learn. Technology is not something separate, but rather integrated into everything we do. It's an extension of our brain. It's who we are.

My dad jokes that my generation would not know what to do if the power went out. What he fails to realize is that we likely have a backup battery. Technology is definitely taken for granted. It would be impossible to cite even just one invention that has changed my generation because there have been so many.

Where technology for previous generations came about to advance industries and lives, the word we have heard for technological innovation is *disruption*. Again and again we have seen technology disrupt and turn industries upside down. For Gen Z growing up, the world's largest taxi company owns no taxis (Uber). The largest accommodations provider owns no real estate (Airbnb). The largest phone companies own no telecommu-

OPRAH WINFREY

In a world so technologically connected . . . what will be the mainstay for your spiritual connection?

61 percent said they are spiritual and 39 percent said they were not.

For those that are spiritual, what is the main way you stay spiritually connected?

TOP 5 ANSWERS

Prayer
Attend place of worship
Read the Bible
Meditation and yoga
Conversations with family and friends

nication infrastructure (Skype). The most popular media owner creates no content (Facebook). The fastest-growing banks have no actual money (SocietyOne). The world's largest movie house owns no cinemas (Netflix).

One big disruption thanks to technology is the job market itself. Gen Z is witnessing the typical first teens' jobs going away. A lot of the companies like fast-food restaurants and amusement parks are now employing machines to sell meals and tickets. On one hand, Gen Z will always have a fear of being automated right out the door. On the other hand, technology is allowing us to create new jobs such as selling things on Craigslist, Etsy, or eBay.

Technology has made most things we do a lot easier. We have access to any bit of information with a push of a button. We also have unlimited access to each other. As mentioned, it has opened the door to how we can even communicate with our icons. If it weren't for technology, there is no way I would have been able to reach out and connect with the amazing icons who contributed questions about Gen Z sprinkled throughout this book.

As we will talk about more, probably the biggest result of growing up in such a high-tech world is that we don't see a line between the physical and digital anymore. They are one and the same. In fact, for every physical element, Gen Z has always seen a digital equivalent. This has changed the landscape for everything from how we shop to how we are educated.

Most of all, it has changed our scope of personal and now professional relationships. We don't see a difference between virtual friends and the ones we know in person.

Wherever they are and however we met them, to us, friends are friends.

Gen Z's Generational Personality

There is no doubt a case can be made that Gen Z has had their own unique events and conditions to shape them. Therefore, they have their very own and different generational personality. Think about a childhood including the Great Recession, the war on terrorism, school shootings, and climate change. And other generations' childhood taboos, such as gay marriage, are now part of Gen Z's norm. Throw in the first black president and the invention of the iPhone and obviously Gen Z will be looking through a new lens.

As Jonah laid out, clearly the world Gen Z has grown up in is rather scary and intense. However, what I love about this next generation is that they are feeling far from defeated. In fact, they are ready to roll up their sleeves and not just fix it, but also put their own stamp on it.

That's why this book is so important. They see their place of employment as one of their main vehicles and partners to make the world a better and prosperous place. The only way we can bring out the best in Gen Z at work is if we understand that they have their very own unique generational personality that will show up at the office.

Will these differences be painful? You bet! Can they be helpful? Of course! But only if we remember that it's not about who is right or wrong, better or worse. It's about accepting the differences and ideally learning how to work with them.

MARK CUBAN

American Businessman and Owner of Dallas Mavericks

How are you different from Millennials (the generation before you)?

TOP 3 RESPONSES

More technologically advanced

More open-minded

Don't care as much about "the norm"

Gen Z is a whole new generation, different from Millennials, Xers, Boomers, and Traditionalists—and that's not a bad thing!

We've talked about what has shaped Gen Z. Now let's dive into the seven resulting traits:

Phigital

Hyper-Custom

Realistic

FOMO

Weconomists

DIY

Driven

PHIGITAL

H-E-L-L-O!

Dad, why are you shouting?

CAN YOU HEAR ME?

They can hear you in Europe! What's your deal?

I'M TALKING ON MY APPLE WATCH! THIS IS SO COOL!

Dad, you must be holding your wrist a millimeter from your face. Put your wrist down and just talk.

HOW WAS YOUR DAY?

You're still shouting. Put the wrist down and just talk.

I couldn't believe I was talking on the phone through my watch. It was crazy. Of course my instinct was to hold it up to my mouth. Why would it feel natural for me to just talk with my watch/phone at my side? But to Jonah it was beyond natural and in fact, it wasn't a big deal at all.

Gen Z lives in a new world where because of rapid advances in technology the barriers between physical and digital have been eliminated. We call it phigital.

Today you can buy something at a store or online. You can write and send a handwritten note or type and send an email. You can work in the office or dial in remotely. And so on. It's great to have options, but they have also sparked many debates. Typically, the goal in these debates has always been to figure out what solution is best—is it physical or is it digital?

The big shift with Gen Z is that we don't see a line at all. What is there to debate?

"Let's Get Phigital"

If you look at how my generation has grown up, technology and connectivity are not things we have had to come to accept: they are part of everyday living, things that we just expect.

I did find it amusing listening to my dad tell me how when he was young if he wanted to go online, he would have to hunt down something called an Internet café. Even crazier is that he would pay to use someone else's computer. For my generation, "logging on" has always meant simply reaching into our pocket for a phone, or glancing down at a watch; before we know it, connecting will mean looking through eyeglasses.

According to Pew Research, in 1995, when the first Gen Zer was born, only 14 percent of U.S. adults had access to the In-

ASHTON KUTCHER
Actor, Entrepreneur, and Activist

Gen X was raised with TV, a largely moderated medium. The Millennials were raised with TV and Internet and in adolescence both of these were very moderated. Gen Z was raised with smartphones and apps and online environments created by users and were largely ungoverned. What are the skills that you believe come with being raised by your curiosity in these unfiltered ecosystems?

TOP 5 RESPONSES

Understanding how it works
Being able to use it, that is, finding anything one needs
Problem solving
Adaptability
Independence

ternet. By 2014 that number was 87 percent. Gen Z has always been connected. More than just connectivity, it's staggering to look at all the digital tools available to them. Consider this: the other generations can remember one, maybe two, big technological advancements during their formative years.

My generation just assumes a big one happens at least every year. Just look at the timeline:

1993: First smartphone was released from IBM and was called Simon.

2000: The first all-in-one device called a smartphone debuts.

2003: Skype launches

2004: Facebook launches

2005: First YouTube Video debuts

2006: Twitter launches and texting is popularized

2007: Apple introduces iPhone

2008: iPhone App Store opens

2010: iPad debuts

2012: iPads go mainstream and start being used in schools

2015: Apple Watch debuts

My generation has only known a world where for every physical element, there is typically a digital equivalent. And it's not an either/or world for us. It's the magical union of both.

We cannot overstate how natural it is for Gen Z to live in a phigital world and just how different that world is. Think about getting directions to somewhere. We all use maps. However, for previous generations, maps were for figuring out which roads were available to you to get to a destination. You would pick the best and fastest way based on your desire to drive highways or side streets. As for how long it would take you to get to your destination, it was a calculated guess.

For Gen Z in the phigital world, we have only had GPS. We still use maps but throw in real-time applications; we also get to see traffic patterns and how people are using the different roads at that exact minute. There is no guessing needed for how long it takes since you get up-to-the-minute calculations of your arrival time. Growing up navigating with GPS, it never occurred to me to use a map that you fold up and keep in the glove box. But that's what my dad always used. Considering how navigationally impaired he is, it's truly amazing he made it around the world in his twenties.

It's not that the other generations don't know how to live in a phigital world; and of course they love to use GPS just as much. It's that Gen Z knows no other world.

Again, we don't see a clear line between the physical and digital, since that suggests they might work against each other. Think about retail. The other generations remember what a big deal it was for brick-and-mortar businesses to have an online presence. The big debate was whether e-commerce would help or hurt their sales.

My generation can't imagine a battle between brick and mortar and online since we see them as one and the same. In fact, Gen Z is witnessing brands that started in the e-commerce world now start to build brick and mortar. Many would assume that my generation just wants to log on and shop. However, our study uncovered that 44 percent of Gen Z would rather shop in-store than online. We like to touch and feel a product, and for a generation with short attention spans, we don't have to wait even a day to get the product if we are willing to go to the store to get it ourselves. That said, for Gen Z, whether you add to your cart in a grocery store or on Amazon .com, it has never mattered.

Warby Parker is a great example of phigital playing out in the marketplace today. They started as an e-commerce business selling eyewear. Their founders saw an opportunity to disrupt the eyewear industry and how eyeglasses were sold. They knew that only 1 percent of eyewear was sold online and were able to leverage the efficiencies of e-commerce by not having rent or physical locations. They had a centralized distribution model and a home try-on program. It was simple. You would order five frames that they would send you in the mail to try on. You would then pick one, order it, and send them back.

"It worked!" said cofounder and co-CEO Dave Gilboa. "We were featured in *GQ* and were called the Netflix of eyewear. However, as much as we could learn about our customers from Google analytics, nothing beat hearing from our customers face-to-face. When we dedicated a small portion of our New York office to retail, suddenly there were hundreds coming to the office every day. We knew we had to expand our model."

Warby Parker started with pop-up shops for eighteen months and eventually opened their first permanent retail location in the SoHo section of Manhattan.

"What we learned," explained Gilboa, "was that our consumers had a relationship with our brand, not a particular channel. Our customer journey includes multiple touch points. For example, a customer could read about us online. Then when they are out and about, they could look us up on their phone and walk into our store to try some glasses on. Then they go home and order a pair online. Most would say that was an online purchase. We don't make the distinction because our customers, especially the younger generations, don't see the difference. The physical and digital worlds not only work together, but ultimately if done right, are one and the same."

The problem is that most businesses are not as forward thinking as brands like Warby Parker. In fact, most are still stuck trying to make a distinction between physical and digital.

When Phigital Shows Up at the Office

Jonah! Where were you?!

What do you mean?

Why weren't you at the meeting?

I was!

Showing up on Skype is not being at the meeting.

Sure it is. The client was fine with it. Why aren't you?

Let me back up. We finally landed a meeting with an HR executive that would open doors to companies for case studies and research on Gen Z, and ideally bring us in to speak on the topic. I explained to Jonah what a great opportunity this was for us and especially for him to network. I was especially excited that I made the meeting for late in the afternoon (after school) so that he could attend.

Yes. My dad was very excited. I looked up the woman on LinkedIn and saw just how connected she was. He must have told me a thousand times that we had to really dazzle her with our cutting-edge research and approach since she gets to see new stuff all the time. As for his pride in making the meeting late in the day, I'm not sure how groundbreaking that is, but I smiled and gave him the thumbs-up.

Now, I will admit that all I gave Jonah was the name of the

client. I assumed he would just enter it into his phone and know where to meet me.

I got to the client's office and before I could even take off my coat she said, "Wow! That son of yours sure is charming. I can't believe he is only sixteen years old. I can see why you want him to be the voice of his generation." I was impressed that he was not only on time, but indeed beat me to the meeting. I was even a little annoyed knowing the jabbing he would give me for being "late."

We walked down the hall and into an empty conference room, at which point I asked, "Where's Jonah?" She said, "Oh, he is joining us via Skype," and proceeded to wave at her laptop on the table. I kid you not, my jaw was resting on my chest. I slowly turned to see Jonah waving back.

Okay. I was mad.

No. He was *really* mad and I'm still not sure why. In the end, the meeting went great and she even hired us to present at their spring meeting. He never said I had to drive downtown to the meeting; he just said that he made it late in the day so I could be there . . . which, again, I was! And for the record, she was pretty impressed with our use of technology—which took care of his other criteria, that we stand out from the crowd. I did nothing wrong and, if you ask me, made an impressive effort—not to mention impression.

We saw this so differently. I will admit Jonah was right. The meeting did go well and we landed a big project. However, in my eyes, it was a risky move. I had spent a lot of time landing the meeting and showing up on Skype could have really backfired. I saw him as almost lazy for not wanting to drive downtown to a meeting.

And in my eyes, I didn't see any risk at all. In fact, I saw it as being efficient and cutting-edge. My dad also needs to give me credit. I called in advance and tested it, and had the connection not worked, I would of course have been there in person.

If it's that hard for us to navigate a simple meeting in the phigital world, how are we ever going to figure out how to work together?

Catching Up in the Workplace

Embracing any digital option has not exactly been an easy or fast process in the workplace. What Xer doesn't remember in the 1990s banging their head against the wall trying to convince leaders to allow employees access to the Internet? All the conversations around how distracting the Internet would become and how access would be seen as an employee benefit that would be monitored. It took a long time for leaders to actually understand that it was a benefit to the organization.

It was the same thing for the Millennials, only this time they weren't banging their heads against the wall for access to the Internet, it was social media. Endless discussions of how Facebook was a distraction at work. According to Robert Half Technology, an IT staffing firm, in 2009, 54 percent of U.S. companies said that they had banned workers from using social networking sites like Twitter, Facebook, LinkedIn, and

MySpace while on the job. It took six years for companies to catch on and by 2015, most had full-time resources dedicated to social media strategies to reach the outside world. Where it was once considered a distraction, Facebook has unveiled Facebook at Work, which lets businesses create their own internal social networks.

My generation can't imagine a day where you couldn't log on to Facebook, Twitter, Snapchat, LinkedIn, and more. It also feels strange that it is groundbreaking for a company to have an internal network that allows the sharing of information and the ability to build relationships and collaborate on a closed social platform. I have been doing this since I assembled my first group text at the age of twelve.

On one hand, Gen Z might just be too far ahead for companies to catch up. Yet on the other, they might just be the perfect solution and the ones to lead the way.

Author Don Tapscott talks about how instead of a generation gap, we actually have a generation lap, where Gen Z is lapping the older ones. As he put it, "This is the first time in history when children are an authority about something really important." Eliminating the line between physical and digital barriers will be paramount to a business's success. These new systems are the exact ones that Gen Z is already "expert" at. It's more than being a digital pioneer. It's about being a digital native. Where Millennials felt criticized for using technology, Gen Z will likely be rewarded and even promoted for it. For Gen Z, being on the bottom rung will not mean what it used to for previous generations. Gen Z's comfort level in the phigital world will make them the hottest candidate for some of today's most in-demand jobs, which did not even exist ten years ago—social media community manager, mobile app developer, or user experience designer, to name a few. Take it one step further. According to a study at Duke University, 65 percent of youth entering school today will work in jobs that do not currently exist.

Again, it looks like Gen Z could be a hot candidate to get in the door, especially as companies navigate between physical and digital worlds. The key, however, will be getting Gen Z to knock.

Phigital Recruitment

Dad, I looked up that gravel company to prepare for our speech and I think they went out of business.

What? That can't be. The head of the association gave me their name. Are you sure you are spelling it right?

Positive.

Why do you think they are out of business?

They haven't updated their website in over five years. The pictures look like they're from the 1800s. If they haven't updated their website, I have to believe they're out of business.

Before we even talk about phigital, let's talk solely digital. I would hope this isn't a surprise, but if a company doesn't have a dynamic presence online with a website at a minimum, in our eyes, it doesn't exist. We are even critical of companies now that aren't active on social media. In fact, our survey found that 91 percent of Gen Z say that a company's technological sophistication would impact their decision to work there. If we are interested in your company, we are going to "creep" you. That means from our LinkedIn connections to Google searches and more we are going to see what we can learn from your online presence. We look for those companies that seem to be on top of their game or at least in the game. Recruiting Gen Z 101: Regardless of how old-line your industry is, you will need to be active online.

Take something like the basic interview. Where we used to often start with a phone interview, now it is not uncommon for applicants to have a Skype interview and meet face-to-face . . . or screen to screen. Aside from saving money on travel, the Skype call can feel as though you're more on the cutting edge. At least for those yelling into an Apple Watch.

For my generation, this won't be seen as cutting-edge. Remember, we've had FaceTime since we were old enough to get a smartphone. We won't even be thinking about the money saved and will be most impressed with the impact on the environment. All my generation hears about is how airline travel is ruining the planet.

Looking ahead, Gen Z is likely to go deeper into the phigital world during the recruiting process. One example is the classic resume. While this will always be a critical tool, many Gen Zers feel that resumes are not an authentic portrait of who they really are. Who doesn't make themselves look good on paper, right? Enter the phigital world and now we are seeing more video resumes. Why just send paper when you can send a short video that gives employers an even more authentic view?

For Gen Z, recruiting in the phigital world looks more like new apps such as JobSnap. You open it up and get to scan a list of jobs. You swipe right or left to accept or reject each one. If you accept, your profile is sent to the employer, who then also swipes right or left to accept or reject. The app matches those looking for work with people who are looking to hire. If you match, the first step is to create a short video and send it in right from your phone. JobSnap doesn't require a resume. Your video is your resume. It's quick, easy, and done right from your smartphone.

Creator Jeff Boodie explains, "We created this specifically for Gen Z, who live and breathe on their mobile devices. We found as this generation was applying for their first job, they were impatient with the grind of the application process. We started with restaurants, retails, and hotels in Southern California that were looking to hire Gen Z. Part of the problem was that these jobs require a level of charisma that employers were struggling to find. It's not like Gen Zers have resumes with tons of bullets. By ditching the traditional resumes and using videos, employers can scan for that charisma they are looking for. More than being quick and easy for Gen Z applicants, employers find it equally as efficient."

Companies such as McDonald's, Panera Bread, Del Taco, Taco Bell, Sears, Forever 21, and American Girl were quick to adopt this phigital approach. In the first three months alone of launching the app, one thousand applicants were matched with jobs.

According to career publisher Vault's annual employer survey, 89 percent of employers revealed that they would watch a video resume if it were submitted to them.

This makes complete sense to Gen Z, since we have been editing and posting videos on YouTube for as long as we can remember. Why wouldn't we do it when we try to get our first job? Our goal would be for the debrief to go like this: "Remember that guy with the video? What about him?"

However, what confuses me is that there are still some who are scared of video resumes for fear of being discriminatory. As we see it, LinkedIn changed the game. We can now go online and not just read about applicants, but see them there, too, anyway. Video makes the application process all the more authentic. That's what Gen Z is looking for. The problem could end up being that Gen Z might think a company is behind if they turn away from something like a video resume. Remember, 91 percent of Gen Z say that a company's technological sophistication would impact their decision to work there.

More than Gen Z's phigital nature redefining how they apply for jobs, it will redefine how they work at the jobs they actually get hired to do.

Work Remotely? Doesn't Everyone?

With the introduction of digital tools like VPN, Skype, and Slack, the idea of where work gets done has truly evolved. The dialogue over working remotely has gone to the next level. Of all the topics I've covered, remote or flexible working arrangements has definitely been a hot button when it comes to the generations.

Gen Z's parents (the Xers) were really the first to fight for remote work arrangements. I remember many Xers entering the workforce and asking for remote and custom work arrangements, which caused big generational collisions with Boomers and Traditionalists. It was just so foreign for competitive Boomers who wouldn't have wanted to be away from the office for fear that they would miss out on a key piece of information or an opportunity for positive exposure.

Independent Xers, on the other hand, liked the idea of stepping away from the office, where internal politics seemed to get in the way and slow things down. Xers have always pushed to do things at their own pace and in their own space. Just tell Xers what you need and when you need it and then they go away, hopefully you go away, and the job gets done. When Xers entered the workforce, thanks to the advent of cell phones, Xers *could* actually step away from the office and still be connected to their jobs. Over the years, as technology has advanced, it has opened the door for more and more unique remote work arrangements. With the arrival of Gen Z, you can bet the dialogue will only continue. However, in some ways parts of the dialogue will actually come to an end while other parts will evolve into all-new discussions and debates.

The difference with my generation is that we aren't necessarily looking to avoid the other generations as much as our Gen X parents were. Because of so many digital tools, we can feel as connected as ever. In fact, we want to be connected. As new tools continually are introduced, we will hopefully lead the way on how best to adopt them and demonstrate to the rest how we can all "show up" regardless of where we are physically.

It's great that Gen Z will be willing to show us the digital tools to work remotely, but at the end of the day, the real gap is one that has been around for decades and lies within the different mindsets of the generations. In my first book, *When Generations Collide*, published in 2002, I wrote about how research showed that those who work remotely weren't respected as much:

> There is a study that was completed by Ceridian Corporation in 1999 called "The Boundaryless Workforce." The Ceridian study found that respondents fifty and over (Traditionalists and Boomers) were more likely to view boundaryless workers as "*less respected than traditional workers.*" This finding not only highlights the most ingrained generational collision getting in the way, but will take the most effort to overturn. We are seeing time and time again that the older generation's model was that those who aren't visible on the plant floor or at their desks are more dispensable. As virtual work options become more commonplace, will older workers be able to truly value a virtual workforce?

As Gen Z enters the workforce we can finally bridge the physical and digital divide. Older generations can embrace the digital options more, and organizations are getting better at knowing how to combine the two, in part aided by Gen Z. The good news for Gen Z is that "older" workers at last can value a virtual workforce. Since Xers are the ones stepping into leadership positions within companies, the mindset will be changed. It's not that Boomers haven't come along; it's that Xers were the original crusaders. With more Xers at the helm, they will understand, embrace, and even respect how Gen Z's phigital mindset will expect boundaryless work arrangements.

It's exciting to imagine that Gen Z won't have to battle or deal with all the discussions around the ability to work remotely. However, all the dialogue so far around working remotely is about defining a line between being at an office or being at home or even a coffee shop. The idea is that the office is home base and there can be outliers that report in.

When you live in a phigital world like Gen Z, that line has been eliminated.

Where's the Office?

Think about how newsworthy it has always been when we see thousands of people gather together in one place—whether it be in Tahrir Square in Cairo or Times Square in New York City.

Now stop and think about how my generation experiences thousands gathering in one place together each day with a hashtag or some online forum. Not only is it not newsworthy, it's not a big deal to us or that different. For Gen Z, virtual is part of our reality. As I've said, for everything that is physical, there is a digital equivalent.

What will this mean for the "office"?

Think about how most traditional offices define their culture. It is usually defined around place, including things such as the office furniture, the color of the paint on the walls, and mostly the overall vibe within those four walls. Sure, a company can have a shared mission and vision, but those with multiple locations will be the first to point out how the culture in one location (more strict and uptight) is different from another (more laid-back and chill).

Over the past fifteen years, as Millennials have trickled and then flooded into the workplace, companies have wanted to create more of a "cool" culture. We saw the shift from "cubicle farms" to more experiential physical work environments. It has been all about open office concept. Companies like Facebook and Google have led the way, leaving many members of the older generations scratching their heads: Is such a workplace an office or an amusement park?

The physical office environment will continue to be an important element when creating a culture, but with the ar-

---

PETE CARROLL
Head Coach of the Seattle Seahawks

How can Gen Z bring people together and how will your talents and ideas contribute to making the world a better place?

TOP RESPONSE: Caring about and respecting one another

---

rival of Gen Z, their phigital mindset will add a layer of complexity.

For Gen Z, culture will have nothing to do with place. We will define culture by who we connect with not just across the hallway, but across the screen as well. Interests or hobbies will define our location as much as physical space. We think it is so cool how companies like Automattic, the company that brought us WordPress, employs more than 430 people distributed across forty countries but does not even have an office. In fact, they don't even use email. This is a company that develops a range of products and services that power 24 percent of all websites on the Internet today and is valued at more than a billion dollars.

Matt Mullenweg, founder and CEO of Automattic, explained: "A key point from our creed is this: 'I will communicate as much as possible, because it's the oxygen of a distributed company.' Our entire system is built on this: we primarily communicate with each other through internal WordPress.com group blogs, called p2's, and we participate in group chat with Slack. Text can be the default, but we've found that voices and faces also help to understand nuance, to share ideas with each other, and to come to agreement on questions or issues. Group video chat has come a long way, whether it's Zoom or Google Hangouts—and I host monthly, livestreamed town hall Q&A sessions with the entire company. Trust comes through our words and our actions—we communicate our trustworthiness through the words we write, the encouragement and help we offer others, the leadership we show in our work and our relationships. When it comes to trust I'm

REBECCA MINKOFF
Cofounder and Creative Director of Rebecca Minkoff

Do you see technology as more of a tool for—or a barrier to—connecting with the people who matter to you?

It is a tool: 84 percent
It is a barrier: 16 percent

not sure that a distributed company is very different than a company in one geographic location. We build trust through doing our best work and helping each other."

Can any Boomer or Xer imagine having had a conversation with their parents like this when they graduated?

"Mom and Dad, I got a new job!"

"Wonderful, honey. Where?"

"Automattic."

"Where are they located?"

"All over. In fact, they are in forty countries!"

"Where's their office?"

"They don't have one."

To a phigital generation like Gen Z, the conversation feels very normal, and in fact, we will likely gravitate to companies like Automattic, where our focus can be on the work we are doing and whom we are doing it with. Location really won't matter. Our office will always just be where our laptop (with stellar webcam), tablet, or smartphone resides.

It's Not What You Say . . . It's How You Say It, or Type It, or Text It

More than just how and where Gen Z works, phigital will also change the way we communicate at work.

Jonah, please send a thank-you note to our client and I don't mean an email or a text.

Dad, who sends snail mail letters anymore?

Exactly! This is why it's a good thing. Do me a favor and try to make it legible. Your handwriting looks like you're in third grade.

Fine, and I'll admit that my writing isn't great, but let me ask you a question . . . What would Thomas Jefferson be saying about your writing? I don't see you exactly pulling out a feather and bottle of ink and writing in calligraphy.

Touché.

Whether it is actual modes or specific words or slogans, communication and generations have been causing gaps for centuries. From *groovy* to *dude* to *YOLO* to *BAE* each generation has its own lexicon. However, with Gen Z communicating in a phigital world, there will be some forces at play that will likely create even more gaps as well as means to communicate.

For my generation, we've been thumbing our way across a variety of screens including phones, laptops, and tablets. My dad makes fun of my handwriting but doesn't realize that it isn't even taught in schools anymore. That doesn't mean we don't see value in writing things down. In fact, Wakefield Research did a study and found that 93 percent of Gen Z believe students who write things down on paper get better grades. But what really frustrates me is that everyone is so quick to accuse my generation of being illiterate or that we don't know how to write. The reality is that we are "writing" more than any other generation. Gen Zers post, comment, and blog more than anyone before. "LOL" or "OMG" might not seem like true writing to some, but in the phigital world, it's still writing.

It's Not Just How You Say It . . . It's How You See It, Too

With screens constantly broadcasting graphics and video at them, it's no surprise that Gen Z is used to a lot of visual stimulation and communication. We have seen the push for more visual communication from the younger generations in the past.

Think back to the 1980s, when *USA Today* debuted. It was the *New York Times* versus *USA Today.* Younger generations liked how *USA Today* would take the same news that in the *Times* was spread out over pages and pages and instead summarize it in a colorful graph with a short paragraph. Even better, there were four-color pictures. *USA Today* capitalized on this with their slogan, "Not the most words, just the right words." Now the quest for communication to come alive continues to expand with Gen Z.

Most companies are figuring this out when communicating externally to customers. However, internal communication hasn't exactly come alive.

Previous generations did see a transition from print-based material to online. However, in Gen Z's eyes, the only result was that the same material that was once printed could now be viewed online. It was just words. Nothing changed except now there was a lot of scrolling. With my generation growing up as the largest consumers of online video, not to mention podcasts, interactive apps, and more, messaging has always come alive. There has been way more than words. Even better, it has always fit perfectly onto our phone screens. Communication that requires us to zoom in and then read and scroll and read and scroll some more not only is far from coming alive, but bores us to death.

Today, with my generation, a good slogan might be "No words

TONY HSIEH
CEO of Zappos

What's one thing that you believe to be absolutely true, that you think older generations may not?

Answers showed a wide range of opinions. Where Generation Z agreed was that everyone should have the right to express themselves in whatever way they might and that men and women should be treated equally.

Where Generation Z differed was on technology. Some felt it was crucial for advancement while others felt it ruins families and is damaging at times.

at all." While Millennials carried the torch when it came to initiating text messaging as the norm, it has been Gen Z who has led the way in using images. We are the emoji generation and in the phigital world we have replaced words with symbols.

Or are they really one and the same? Case in point is the famous "Word" of the Year for Oxford Dictionaries. In 2015, the "word" was 😂. It was the emoji for "tears of joy" and wasn't even a word at all in the traditional sense.

Oxford had partnered with mobile technology firm SwiftKey and uncovered that the most used emoji was the face "tears of joy." Upon announcing this selection, there was a big uproar.

In an interview, the president of Oxford Dictionaries, Casper Grathwohl, told us that they anticipated not only a reaction, but also one that was generational in nature.

"Not surprising, the Gen Zers were the most excited about the selection. We anticipated that Xers, Boomers, and Traditionalists would have a negative reaction and they did account for a lot of the chatter," he said. "They really challenged us on whether or not this was a word." Casper went on to share that they went with the emoji because it was a word that best reflected the ethos, mood, and preoccupations of 2015. As he explained, "We wanted to draw out a conversation that communication is changing today, and that we did!"

Oxford Dictionaries is right, communication is shifting today, especially in our personal lives. Much of the shift is being stewarded by Gen Z. In fact, Gen Z is mentoring family and friends on how best to use emojis and especially not to over-emoji. Nothing will get a Gen Zer to roll their eyes more than when they get a text from one of their parents with six thumbs-up, four party hats with streamers, and eleven hearts.

The challenge, however, is that as Gen Z enters the workplace, they will continue to steward the change. It's one thing sending an emoji to mom or dad; it's another communicating this way to coworkers, bosses, or even clients. This could open the door for many conflicts and generation gaps with Gen Z.

Traditionally, communication at work has been very formal. The goal in communicating has always been to eliminate ambiguity. The more precise you could be, the better. Any straying from formal or standard communication would be perceived as giving up that precision and, in many ways, even respect.

One thing is for sure, there wasn't a lot of room for emotions. The only way to express an emotion when writing was the dreaded ALL CAPS. IF YOU WROTE IN ALL CAPS, THAT IMPLIED YOU WERE SHOUTING OR MAD. Sure, you could *italicize* or **bold** the text, but that only emphasized a word—it didn't express an emotion.

At Virgin Hotels, they rolled out an internal app called VSocial to share information as well as create a platform for team members to communicate with each other. Clio Knowles, vice president of people at Virgin Hotels, explained: "Technically it worked great and everyone loved having it. However, the more the team, especially our Gen Zers, started to communicate with each other, they told me that they were having trouble with formal-based communication. I thought texting each other would be enough, but it wasn't. I learned that it wasn't authentic enough for Gen Z. They wanted to have emojis. It wasn't enough to tell a teammate they were doing a good job; they needed to add a thumbs-up. So naturally for version 2.0 we added emojis."

With emojis and more visual communication, the door will be kicked wide open for expressing not only more emotion at work, but definitely a lot of ambiguity as well.

Imagine a simple note to the boss: "Sent the document to the client 😂."

What if the boss wasn't hip to knowing it signified "tears of joy"? Is the boss to assume you're not sure about what you sent? Sad about it? That you're nervous you haven't heard back? That it didn't go well?

> My concern is that everyone will accuse Gen Z of being unprofessional or immature, when in reality, we feel we can improve communication in the business world. For example, telling a new client, "We are thrilled to receive your business," can be all the more exciting by simply adding 👍 😀 🤝; just don't do all three. Why not send a video of the office staff cheering and thanking the new client? Sure, it might not be as formal as in the past, but by personalizing communication through some emotion and visual stimulation, Gen Z will feel it is all the more authentic.

Just as companies had to write new entries for the employee handbook covering social media usage when Millennials showed up, the same will be true for Gen Z's communication in the phigital world. We cannot assume Gen Z will innately know that they probably shouldn't send "u" instead of "you" to a client.

Or a video of workers dancing that could be a bit over-the-top. They will also have to be mentored that by not spelling something out—literally—and instead using an emoji or graphics, they could leave others more confused than clear on what they meant to say. Sometimes the most words will be the right words and at other times, communicating the Gen Z way will be 👌.

Face-to-Face: Some Things Will Never Change

As we all learn about Gen Z operating in a phigital world, it will only be natural to assume that if you want to connect with us, you should send us a text—ideally with more emojis than words. Gen Z is so comfortable with our digital tools, who wouldn't assume this? However, it would be a dangerous assumption to make.

One of our favorite findings from our national survey, since it even surprised us, was that when it came to how Gen Z wanted to communicate at work, face-to-face was by far the front-runner. Eighty-four percent of Gen Z prefer communicating face-to-face with a boss and 78 percent of Gen Z prefer communicating face-to-face with a peer.

Just because your own Gen Z kids don't answer your call and prefer to text you, that doesn't mean your Gen Z employee will feel the same way. My generation craves human interaction. If leaders just assume that the best way to communicate is to text us, then they will miss out on developing the working relationship we want to have at work. If you can't be in the same room, then still FaceTime or Skype us.

SETH ROGEN
Actor and Comedian

What makes you happy?

TOP 5 RESPONSES
Being with other people
Doing things I love
Smiling
Love
Financial stability

By avoiding face-to-face communication with Gen Z we would miss out on helping them to develop real and authentic communication. There is something to be said for learning how to communicate on your feet, to be quick and savvy in responding, or having to live with the first words out of your mouth. If everything they communicate is edited or touched up, then they won't learn about genuine conversations. Many experts are worried about Gen Z not learning the art of conversation because the digital world has made communication so calculated. They will need to learn that there is an art to listening and responding in real time, and that in life, you don't always get to take things back or make them perfect. The good news is that they are hungry for these genuine conversations. The bad news is that the other generations assume Gen Zers aren't interested and will just send a text.

When we went over the finding that Gen Z is most interested

in face-to-face communication with fellow Gen Zers, most were not surprised at all. In fact, the feelings were unanimous. There were two big forces at play. First, we spend so much of our time sifting through digital messaging, whether it's a text, a post, a digital ad, or an online video. More than just consuming all this messaging, we have to also learn to figure out what we can and cannot trust. What is truly a real message and what is a marketing scam or made up? In addition, Gen Zers told us that growing up in a time of so much uncertainty has really emphasized the need to develop relationships that you can trust. These two forces have led us to put a premium on face-to-face communication. We want leaders to look us in the eye and want to be able to look back at them. The bottom line is that there are some things that we will never have an app for and human connection is one of them.

And then there are some things that we never dreamed we would have an app for . . . but now do.

Jonah! I just got the nicest thank-you note from the meeting planner commenting on how impressed she was to get a handwritten note from you.

Nice!

You see? It does make a difference and is worth the time.

You're definitely right. I never imagined we would be getting thank-you emails for our handwritten thank-you notes. Kind of weird, but it works.

She really gushed about it, too. I'm so impressed that I didn't have to remind you. What did you say? You usually show me the notes before we send them. I didn't know you even knew how to address the envelope and find a stamp.

Very funny, Dad. Actually, I found this killer website called bond.co. You type up what you want and who it goes to and email it to them. Then for three dollars they handwrite and send the note for you. Businesses are using them all the time because like you said, handwritten notes make a difference.

You're kidding, right?

No! I read that financial planners and Realtors are using them so I figured if they are, then we definitely can. By the way, I'm glad you reminded me about this: You owe me three bucks.

Phigital at its finest.

Phigital Zingers!

- Watch for Gen Z to combine the physical with the digital in how they consume, live, and work.
- Consider recruiting tools that combine the digital with the physical, such as Skype, JobSnap, and more.
- Use digital tools for remote work as ways to stay connected, not disconnect.
- Put phigital solutions to work to enhance and spread organizational culture.
- Be open to new additions to the lexicon—they may be visual, video, or even symbolic; all of them can enhance communication.
- Never underestimate the value Gen Z still places on face-to-face interaction.

HYPER-CUSTOM

Dad, Gramps got me a Kanye CD for my birthday.

That's nice.

Kind of a waste, don't you think?

Why? I thought you liked Kanye.

I do, but not all of his songs. I wish Gramps had given me an iTunes gift card so I could just build my own playlist.

My dad remembers buying CDs with the understanding that you won't like all of the songs, but hopefully a lot of them. My generation makes our own playlists and YouTube videos, posts photos, mashes up music, creates multimedia presentations, and develops personalized content. This has launched companies like SoundCloud, Spotify, and iHeartRadio.

Like all the generations, Gen Z has had to deal with the

teenage angst of figuring out the game of fitting in while still wanting to show how they are unique. Some things just never change. However, what has evolved for Gen Z is that it has gotten a lot easier to truly showcase what makes you stand out from the crowd. Gen Z has grown up in one hyper-custom world.

Ask a Boomer how they let the world know what made them unique and odds are it was the patches that were sewn onto their jean jacket. Ask an Xer and it was the mixtape they created that definitely took a lot longer to make than a few clicks of the mouse.

For my generation, from Twitter handles to Instagram posts to Facebook pages, we have always had tools at our fingertips to help us identify and customize our own personal brand for the world to know. It's super-easy! All someone has to do is look at my feed and within seconds they will know that I love to compete at CrossFit and snowboarding, wear preppy brands, worship the Minnesota Vikings, like rap and country, love Elon Musk, and have an insane infatuation with Gen Z. If I wake up one day and decide I don't like Elon Musk, I simply hit "delete." I don't have to rip off a patch and leave a hole in my jacket. All these tools at our disposal have allowed us to customize our personal brand at a young age.

From media to politics and beyond, Gen Z has unprecedented ability to select and control their preferences. This is a wonderful thing when it comes to empowerment.

In addition, Gen Z has grown up in an era of acceptance and support that has encouraged them to customize their personal brand and share it with the world. A lot of things on Gen

MUHTAR KENT
Former Chairman and CEO of the Coca-Cola Company

What qualities will you bring to the table that previous generations haven't?

TOP 3 RESPONSES
Technological ability
Open-mindedness
Determination

Z's profiles today, for example, would not have been as easy for a Boomer to wear as a patch on a jean jacket.

Take something like homosexuality. It is a lot more common to see a teen posting the rainbow symbol today than it would have been for a Boomer or even Xer as a teen. That's not to say there still isn't work to be done when it comes to acceptance in this country.

What Box Do I Check?

There is no denying that there has been tremendous progress over the years when it comes to workplace diversity. With each new generation, there seems to be more of a push for acceptance. Gen Z will be no different. In fact, 77 percent of Gen Z says that a company's level of diversity affects their decision to work there.

The thing to get excited about is that for this hyper-custom generation, their definition of diversity will be pushed to new limits, or should we say, beyond limits. Gen Z has been so focused on creating their own individual brands that it has allowed identity to be more customized than ever before. Growing up, I remember that there were five boxes to check to define yourself: White, Black, Asian, Hispanic, or Other.

If these were the choices for my generation today, a majority of us would check "Other." I would want to also check that I'm a Jewish, straight, Gemini, ENTJ CrossFitter. How we define ourselves is so customized that there could never be enough boxes for us to check. Facebook, for example, has fifty different gender designations, so it will feel limiting to go to work and not have more boxes to check.

We aren't as likely to fall into typical categories and are more likely to mix and match. Self-identification is just too customized. It is awesome to see so many companies have affinity groups since it does provide a place to belong, meet people who are similar, and even feel a sense of safety. However, Gen Z will want to take that even further and create more of them as well as belong to many of them and not just one. Beyond just race, gender, or religion, we will include interests, hobbies, points of view, and even generation. This is something that I hope leaders will let my generation lead the way on.

Gen Z's hyper-customization goes beyond just showcasing their own brand for the world to know. It works the other way around, where brands and experiences have always been customized for them.

The Amazon Effect

Jonah, let's stop at Foot Locker and get some shoes.

No thanks. I'll do it at home.

Why? We are right here. It won't take long.

They don't have what I want.

How do you know? You said you wanted Nikes and I know they carry them.

They do, but I want to design my own pair. It doesn't cost that much more. I just go to Nike.com and I can pick the color for everything from the sole to the laces to the Nike swoosh.

Thanks to the collection of big data, the online retail experience for Gen Z has created an expectation that marketers will have an intimate understanding of their behaviors and desires.

I love how when I log on to Amazon it says in big bold letters, "Welcome Back, Jonah." It then asks me how I liked my recent purchase of exercise socks. Even better, it asks me if I would be interested in a pair of shorts to match. How cool is that? I can't help but think that Amazon knows me. We just assume that companies know us and can talk to us on this intimate level. This is something that colleges and universities had to pick up on as Gen Z went to college.

No longer is the standard acceptance letter with "insert name here" working to get my generation to join the incoming freshman class. Iowa State, for example, sends out a link that launches a personalized video with a CNN reporter announcing the big news that this applicant has been accepted to the school. With dramatic music, graphics, and all, the Gen Z applicant's name is in lights. It not only is customized, but really exciting and entertaining.

This level of customization has carried over into the college experience itself.

What Did You Say Your Major Was?

For the rest of us, when it came to declaring our college major, you pretty much picked from a standard list of options and checked the box. For a lot of hyper-custom Gen Zers, they don't want to check any box and instead want to fill in the blank. In other words, they want to customize their own major. After all, that's what they did with their playlists, right? Northeastern University found that 72 percent of Gen Z believe that colleges should allow students to design their own course of study or major. Many institutions have been responding and offer the option to create an individualized major with the help of an academic counselor.

Some may think that customizing your own major is an opportunity to create an easier path to graduation. On the contrary, it is a rigorous journey that involves an extensive approval process followed by check-ins with benchmarks along the way. Probably the one doing the most work is the college or university in catering to this customization.

Joshua Hatch, senior editor for data and interactives at the *Chronicle of Higher Education*, commented, "Higher education tends to be more service oriented today. The mindset is that students are customers. This is good and bad. The good is that universities are asking themselves, 'How can we best service the students?' On the flip side, it makes it challenging for faculty to properly evaluate students. If the student performs poorly, the student can claim they were not properly served."

So if online experiences like Amazon or the colleges we attend can create these personal experiences that really make us feel that they know us, it would be only natural for my generation to expect this level of customization when we hit the workplace.

The Customization Continuum at Work

Customization in the workplace has evolved through the generations. For Traditionalists entering the workforce, the focus was on professionalizing and creating structure. It was the era of the assembly line, where the only customization in your job was what task you had on the plant floor or what shift you worked. If you worked in the office, there were distinct departments. In addition, there were precise ladders that laid out the path to the top. Again, the only customization was what rung you were on.

Thankfully these specific structures were in place by the time 80 million Boomers arrived, so they would know exactly what their title and pay grade were as well as where they landed on the ladder. On one hand, Boomers had to fit into the structure. Yet on the other hand, they had to figure out a way to stand out among 80 million. From your personality to the hours you put in to how you made yourself visible on an assignment, Boomers customized their style so that they could be noticed and hopefully promoted up the ladder.

When Xers showed up and really balked at the strict structure, they couldn't help but stand out. Unfortunately, it was not in a good way. Climbing the ladder didn't mean as much because they had seen too many before them pay too big a price for success. Customization was focused on creating your independence even if that meant not fitting into the structure. Institutions like government and the military saw a lot of attrition with Gen X because there was just too much structure and no room for independence. Many Xers turned to the ultimate customization by starting their own businesses. Because they were much smaller in size, at 60 million, it didn't feel as risky. As 80 million Boomers moved up and out, Xers felt that they could always get a job.

When 82 million collaborative Millennials showed up, they had what many called a pack mentality. Unlike independent Xers, Millennials were more focused on their teams. They believed they were only as strong as their weakest link and so they banded together to get the job done. They didn't feel as much pressure to customize on the job since they had their social networks outside work in which to express themselves.

Now comes Gen Z, and we will have big expectations about customizing to our needs and desires. First of all, we've been spending so much time building our personal brand that we want our employers to leverage it. Let's say, for example, that part of your personal brand is you love to design infographics. Even if you're not applying for a job in the creative department, you would hope your employer would look for ways to build infographics into your job description. Too often companies only ask your name, where you went to college, past work experience, and your marital status. We want to share more and hope employers will ask. I think it's so cool that at Virgin Hotels they have their own internal network, like Facebook, where employees all have their own pages. They post information about themselves, including their favorite songs, sounds, cool nicknames, etc. Basically the company wants to know what your personal brand is all about. And Gen Z wants to share it.

As I said, we will have expectations around customization. From job titles to career paths to training and development to feedback and more, we will want it all customized. One thing I worry about is being labeled as entitled. I understand how it could be perceived that way in that the other generations hiring and managing us weren't asking for this level of customization. The problem is that "entitlement" has a lot of negative reactions. It often leads to conversations about not being willing to work hard to get ahead or that you expect things to be handed to you sooner than deserved. Our push for customization has nothing to do with our willingness to work hard and we for sure have learned that nothing comes easy. This is not about a sense of entitlement but it is all about the realities of the world we have grown up in. As I mentioned, everyone from Amazon to our colleges has been customizing to our needs so it will feel only natural that our employers would be willing to customize. However, if this assumption leads to labels like "entitled" then we are going to start off on the wrong path. Our hope is that pushing for customization on the job will be good for all employees in leveraging their personal brands as well as good for companies. Granted, one could easily argue that it's too cheesy for corporate America to send out a CNN video offering a new recruit a job, but there is no denying that customization has gone to a whole new level.

Hello. My Title Is ___________.

Dad, the guy that is introducing us has the coolest job.

What is it?

Experience Ninja.

Are you kidding?

No, I'm not. Here, look at his business card.

What does he do?

He said he fights to figure out the best experience for their customers and partners. I think that sounds awesome.

So, basically he's in customer service.

This generation is not going to be jazzed about signing up for a job with a title that everyone else seems to have. So rather than roll our eyes at them, maybe we should roll with them.

If you can create your own profile with names, nicknames, or hashtags, it makes all the sense in the world that you should be able to create your own job title, right? It's not about being cute or even funny; it's about customizing your job so it feels like it belongs specifically to you. If the responsibilities are the same, then is a custom title that big a deal? To Gen Z, it just might be. In fact, having our own custom title could make us feel more empowered.

That's exactly what Michael Biggerstaff, CEO of the digital marketing firm Nxtbook Media, discovered. He lets his employees pick their own job title. First he has his new hires spend a month in their job. Then the firm sits down with them and asks them to design their own title. "We want them to really get a feel for what it is they do and then tell us what they think they should be called," explains Michael. "We find we can create a better connection between the employee and their role. Also, by coming up with their own title, their job stays more top of mind every day."

The person who trains customers on the software being licensed is the "Rocket Science Educator." The office manager? "Master of Smooth Solutions." When the sales manager realized that he was selling more than just products and services after a month on the job, he decided to be called the "Duke of Solutions." As for Michael himself, he sees his role as inspiring his staff to be the best they can be. Therefore, he doesn't go by "CEO" and instead is "Chief Inspiration Officer."

Biggerstaff said the younger generations seem to gravitate to the ability to customize their job titles and that some Xers and Boomers struggle with it. As he explained, "We don't make people come up with something funky if they don't want to. For a lot of Boomers and Xers, they've worked hard and competed with peers to land titles such as director or supervisor. It is more important to them to have a traditional title. That's fine, too."

"One thing is for sure," he went on. "Creating custom job titles has been amazing for us in recruitment. When recruits hear about customizing their title, it's the tip of the iceberg for them wanting to learn more about our culture. It sets the tone for flexibility to how work gets done, which is something we are proud of."

Recruitment goes beyond just employees. Michael uses custom titles to help recruit clients as well. "I challenge anyone who tells me that they can't do it because their industry is too conservative or clients wouldn't like it. In fact, I tell them it has the opposite effect. What we find is that as soon as you tell someone you are the Duke of Solutions or hand them a business card that says 'Rocket Science Educator' it opens the door for more questions and deeper conversations about what we do and how we can truly help."

So step one is to think about how you can hyper-customize what a job is even called. But step two goes even deeper. Gen Z will also want to customize the job descriptions. In fact, our national study uncovered that 56 percent of Gen Z would rather write their own job description than be given a generic one. Again, this has nothing to do with entitlement. This is about each of us believing we bring unique skill sets to the table. Why let a prewritten job description leave some of our best skills off the table? This will definitely change the recruitment process altogether. Rather than post a specific job description, recruiters will have to post broader needs that will hopefully pique Gen Z's interest to walk in the door. Then once in the door, Gen Z can sit with the employer and customize the ideal, win-win job description.

Let's be clear: The goal isn't to give all control over to Gen

Z to write whatever job description they want. There are needs to be met. The goal in letting Gen Z write some of the job description is to nurture their need for hyper-customization and ideally create more ownership. In addition, as mentioned later in the "DIY" chapter, Gen Z has a lot of skills that are likely being used on the side but that could go unnoticed at work. As Jonah said, if Gen Z is helping to craft the job description, there is a better chance that those skills will be put on the table and put to use for the company. Likewise, weak spots may be uncovered that can be addressed up front through coaching or training.

So we've customized the job title and even the description. However, Gen Z's need for hyper-customization doesn't stop there. It only continues once Gen Z dives into their jobs.

Choose Your Own Adventure

Growing up, one of my favorite memories was of bedtime when my dad would read to me the popular children's game books, Choose Your Own Adventure. I loved having the role of the hero and making choices that would determine how the story ended. Now that my generation is growing up, we will want to continue to "choose our adventure." Our national study found that 62 percent of Gen Z would rather customize their own career plan than have the organization lay one out for them.

Laying out any prescribed career path with exact titles in boxes will feel as foreign as a fax machine to Gen Z. However, pushing back on prescribed career paths has been happening for a while now. In fact, it was Gen Z's parents, the

MARTIN LUTHER KING III

Civil Rights Activist and Eldest Son of MLK Jr.

Do you think there is a difference between management and leadership?

Yes: 85 percent

No: 15 percent

For those who think there is a difference, what is the core difference between management and leadership?

TOP 3 RESPONSES

Leadership is a quality . . . management is a position or role.

Leaders do . . . managers tell.

Leaders inspire and empower workers . . . managers give orders.

Xers, who started it all. Xers balked at a lot of the Boomer structure and bureaucracy and wanted to customize their own career path.

Some industries, such as law and accounting, really struggled because there had only been one path. You started as a summer intern, moved on to associate, then director, and then worked hard to someday be made partner. As Xers and Millennials saw what it really took to become a partner, they made it clear that it wasn't worth it to them.

Traditionalists and Boomers were stuck because this was the only way they knew how to develop and motivate a workforce. Plus, their financial models were all based on a tiered structure of hourly rates. They had to figure out, if Xers didn't want to be partners, how would they achieve maximum value to the firm? With application and attrition rates being threatened, these traditional industries had to adjust. Now, with titles like "contributor" emerging rather than "partner," career paths can be more customized.

This is a good thing because along comes my generation and our hyper-custom mindset will have us just assuming that career paths are one-of-a-kind and personalized. Traditional industries like accounting are definitely catching on as they try to recruit Gen Zers to be summer interns. For example, PricewaterhouseCoopers (PwC) is all about custom career paths. They know that in order to pull in my generation they have to break the stereotype that there is only one path to success. I'm sure Baby Boomers or Gen Xers applying years ago would never have imagined that PwC's college recruitment would state:

> At PwC, we understand how important the first steps outside of college are for your career and recognize our responsibility in helping you reach your long-term career goals—whether at PwC or beyond. That's why we work with you to design your own path, because you are truly the only person who knows what is best for your career.

Companies that have been on the front lines of hiring Gen Z have learned that custom career paths are a must. Kathy Watkins, vice president of learning and development for Panera Bread, explained: "It used to be that you came to work at Panera as a retail associate and there were six steps to make it to assistant manager. It was very linear and prescribed. What we saw with Gen Z was that they wanted to each be seen as their own individual and actually resented conversations that grouped them together. Now when we sit down with a new hire our goal is to talk about all the different career opportunities from the bakery to catering to delivery to manufacturing to our support centers. We want to work with them to design their own custom paths. It may be more work for us up front, but Gen Z will be more engaged and take more ownership because the job feels like it was customized to what they are looking for."

There are pros and cons in Gen Z expecting to hyper-customize their career paths. For starters, consider that Duke University study we mentioned in Phigital that reported that 65 percent of Gen Z entering school today will work in jobs that do not currently exist. We won't have a choice but to learn how to customize career paths since they will navigate through places we have never been. Rather than take on the burden of figuring it out for Gen Z, enlisting their help could be just what we need.

Another upside with Gen Z's focus on hyper-custom career paths is that they won't run into the same situation that their Xer parents did. With so many Boomers in the workforce, many of the top rungs have always been taken. Xers who have worked for organizations that have prescribed paths up the ladder are looking at the rungs above them and realizing that there is nowhere else for them to go. With the reality that Boomers are working and living longer, Xers know that they will be sitting at their rung for a long time. You've never seen an Xer get so excited when a Boomer walks into the office looking sick, tired, or burned out. Kidding aside, Xers have reached what we call the "Gray Ceiling."

With Millennials' population being larger than Gen Z's, this type of situation could repeat itself. However, with Gen Z's eyes on customizing their own path, they might not even notice or feel stuck. They'll simply choose their own adventure and customize a path that goes in all directions to other rungs and ladders or even companies. They will avoid the gray ceiling because they won't see one.

Finally, an upside to more hyper-custom career paths is that managers can really focus on results that match the individual, not just a position. Too often with job descriptions and career paths being so similar over the years, managers get stuck in the fairness game. What they do for one employee, they have to do for another. What they fail to realize is that "fairness" and "equality" are different. Of course you want to

MARTIN SHEEN
Actor

In one word only, what is the essential characteristic of a leader?

TOP RESPONSE: Fairness

treat everyone fairly, but it's also okay to acknowledge that not everyone is equal in skill sets. The more customized a career path is, the more employees can be pushed to hit results that truly match their capabilities and not be lumped together with everyone else.

The downside to Gen Z's push for hyper-customized career paths is that previous generations might not know how to react or evaluate them. A potential employer could evaluate a resume where someone started as an intern, moved to associate manager, then to supervisor, then to regional vice president, and be able to assess whether he or she is ready (or not) to become senior vice president.

However, if this same potential employer looked at a resume where someone started as Experience Ninja, then became Data King, and then Retail Rockstar, the employer might struggle to know if the next step is assistant manager. This custom resume could be one of the most dynamic resumes to come across the desk, but because it is so customized, it would be hard to know how the applicant would fit into a more traditional structure, or even if they should be taken seriously.

This leads to the other downside to hyper-custom career paths, which goes beyond confusion to the issue of respect. Many Xers and Millennials who chose to customize the traditional path weren't always applauded, but instead were questioned. Even if it wasn't said out loud, they could hear, "You don't want to be partner? What is wrong with you?"

The challenge is that Gen Z definitely applauds custom career paths and when they encounter a company that doesn't embrace them, they will now be the ones saying, "What is wrong with you?"

So we get them in the door, we figure out their job title, description, and one-of-a-kind career path, and now it's time to teach them a thing or two. What happens when hyper-customization hits training and development?

Training the YouTube Generation

Hey. I found you a great two-day workshop on Apple Keynote to take. It's over a weekend. I'll go with you if you want.

Do I have to?

You said you would take over building our Keynote presentations. I know PowerPoint, but I don't know Keynote.

I will. But we don't have to go to a two-day class.

Then how are you going to learn how to do it?

I'll watch some YouTube videos and if I can't figure it all out, I'll go to the Apple Store for a one-on-one.

When it comes to learning, Gen Z sees having a lot of information being thrown at us to memorize as a waste of time. Gen Zers progress in a task until we get stuck and need to know something. Then we seek out the information to get unstuck and continue with the task at hand. Our focus is on learning how to find, interpret, and take advantage of information on a need-to-know basis. Bottom line: Gen Z is a generation that has been able to customize its searches to get the exact information we need and nothing more to get a task done.

There is definitely something to be said for not throwing loads of information at Gen Z to memorize. It is likely more efficient to instead let them jump in and try. If they need to know something, they can stop and learn. However, this focus on task-oriented learning does not account for Gen Z obtaining a deeper knowledge of how things work or seeing a bigger picture of how all the smaller tasks work together. The key will be to find a balance of giving Gen Z context to what they are doing while also allowing for a more custom approach to learning all the details.

We will struggle to sit with herds of employees listening to long lessons together at the same pace. Our national study found that one in ten Gen Zers claim they would rather read the full iTunes terms and conditions than attend formal workplace training. It has nothing to do with our passion to learn. In fact, Gen Z will be hungry to learn new skills that can help us get ahead with our careers. It is more about not having to learn via long, lecture-based training with no room for customization.

Gen Z will push for more of a learn-on-the-job approach, where we are put in real-world scenarios and when faced with something we need to know, we stop and learn. When we start our jobs, we will want to just dive right in. When we need to know something, we will stop and learn it, and then move on. A lot of company orientations can go on for days, if not weeks. In our national survey, 56 percent of Gen Z thinks onboarding should take a day or less.

Technology has definitely transformed the way we learn. We can watch a YouTube tutorial and hit play, stop, fast-forward, or rewind. In other words, we can customize when something is being taught, and most important, the pace at which it is taught. We are also accustomed to customizing how material is presented. If you learn better by some guy talking to you, that's the video you click on. If you learn better by graphics, odds are there is that version, too.

However, it's a mistake to assume that everything needs to take place through technology and videos. Don't forget, as our survey uncovered, 84 percent of Gen Z prefers face-to-face communication. We are hungry for it. We still want that two-way human interaction. Not just with instructors, but with each other as well. You can't exactly bounce an idea off YouTube.

Our study also found that 73 percent of Gen Z would like to be taught one-on-one. The problem is that there will never be enough resources or time for all of us to get private tutoring on the job. Perhaps the ideal training situation would be a more phigital

BRIAN NICCOL

CEO of Taco Bell

How can employers help ensure you have the skills and training you need?

TOP 3 RESPONSES

Provide a coach and mentor to guide me to the right resources

Provide internal development opportunities

Provide tuition assistance for external development opportunities approach, with a combination of face-to-face and technological tools. We could learn the basic material at our own custom pace on a computer, and take any tests that we need to complete. Then we could be provided opportunities to meet in person one-on-one to ask custom questions, dig deeper, and, most important, learn the context as to how it all applies to our specific jobs.

One smart move that Panera made with the onset of Gen Z employees was to break down their training into smaller chunks. Gen Zers have an eight-second attention span. In addition, Gen Z is used to getting their information in sound bites. Kathy Watkins explained: "Prior generations could listen to at least five straight minutes of content, but not Gen Z. We lose them a lot quicker. Rather than train them in one long, arduous training session, we broke the curriculum down into as many smaller pieces as possible. We found that Gen Z remained more interested. Also, by breaking it down, they felt more accomplishments along the way, rather than one big sigh of relief that it was over." The other revamp made to their training program to cater to Gen Z is exactly what Jonah was talking about. They used the perfect combination of e-learning and in-person training. Trainees would take a small module on the computer and then immediately be put next to an associate trainer to work with them hip to hip. "This model of study, practice, study, practice was perfect for Gen Z," said Watkins. "They learn something quickly and we keep their attention. Then they get to actually try it right away and we are able to get them excited and confident. As much as they appreciate our e-learning modules, they definitely love the personal connection. Our trainers are able to validate that they are actually learning it and are able to make any corrections earlier on before the employee develops bad habits that take longer to correct."

Whether it is a formal learning and development department or a directory of skill sets around the office, Gen Z will want to have access to mentors who can help answer their custom questions. Before bosses panic that now their whole day will feel like a classroom, Gen Z, as we learn in "DIY," will not assume that the only place to get an answer is the boss. They are open to getting help from anyone who knows. After all, they have grown up with more resource centers in schools, online and offline tutors, even an influx of guidance counselors all available to address their specific needs or fill in the gaps.

So Enough About Me. Let's Talk About My Performance.

The definition of what it means for feedback and reviews to be customized has definitely evolved over time. For Traditionalists, the most customized the feedback got was in how loud you were being yelled at. After all, their model was that if no one was yelling at you, then things were just fine.

For 80 million competitive Baby Boomers, that was not going to be enough. They needed some system to evaluate everyone and ultimately rank them so they knew who could be promoted and who needed to develop more. Therefore, annual employee reviews appeared. There were lots of forms filled out with different sections and matrices so Boomers could get a custom score on how they were doing. This score then determined what the raise would be.

When skeptical Gen Xers came along, that was not customized enough. They weren't as concerned with hearing an exact score since that felt too quantitative. They wanted more customized, *qualitative* information so they could get more than just a number for their performance. In addition, once a year was not going to cut it. Xers couldn't understand why they had to wait to hear about their performance months after they had completed a project.

If the feedback wasn't great, they were left feeling that they had wasted months in which they could have already been working on it and improving. Thanks to Xers pushing back and asking for more, we now have semiannual reviews that are more qualitative in nature. Feedback feels more personal and customized.

When Millennials came along, they loved how feedback was more qualitative. They were used to detailed conversations with their parents about how they were doing. The problem was that most of those conversations were all about good news—all the ways Millennials were excelling. With that hearty boost to their self-esteem Millennials were not ready for the bad news when they showed up at work. Boomers and Xers who were used to delivering constructive or negative input at an employee review were taken back at how much it threw Millennials for a loop. What was just part of a normal review for Boomers or Xers felt more than just personal to Millennials—it felt new and often shocking. They were not used to negative feedback and so extra time had to be spent reassuring Millennials that they were just fine. That said, after a few reviews, Millennials adapted. Also, as they went through a few rounds of feedback on the job, they pushed customization even further. For starters, they were fine with the semiannual reviews, but didn't stop there. They didn't want feedback to just be about formal sit-downs. They were known for knocking on their boss's door every day just to check in on how they were doing. This was an adjustment for those managing them; they would often complain that giving Millennials feedback had become a full-time job. Often managers had to set boundaries and even negotiate how often feedback could happen on the job. Customized feedback for Millennials was also about casting a wider net in terms of who was giving it. The standard practice for years had been that your boss was the one to deliver your report card on the job. However, this collaborative cohort wanted feedback to include not only bosses, but peers, other department heads, mentors, and maybe even customers to get an even more customized report card.

Now my generation will expect feedback to be all the more hyper-customized. What does that mean? We will want our feedback to be even more frequent than daily, easily accessible at our fingertips, and especially broken down project by project, task by task.

The Modern-Day Report Card

Gen Z's notion of being monitored on the job is on a different plane than the rest of us. For other generations, "monitoring progress" meant that in between a formal review you would receive the occasional comment. If you did something great, hopefully someone noticed and said something. And if you didn't do so well, odds were you'd definitely be told. These comments would eventually come together as a one- or two-page summary used for those annual or semiannual sit-downs.

Say "monitoring" to my generation and we think of a world where your parents monitor you 24/7 through your smartphone. They know if you really are at your friend's house. We think of going to Disney and wearing an RFID bracelet that monitors our whereabouts at all times. We think of how iTunes monitors our purchases and makes recommendations.

Gen Z feels we are being monitored for every little thing we do, every minute of the day. We also know that the information is being recorded at all times. Where other generations have felt it is highly invasive, we've just grown accustomed to it. Our national study found that 65 percent of Gen Z is already comfortable being monitored in some fashion or another at work.

As a result, when Gen Z comes to work, this level of custom monitoring will have them assuming that everything they do is being tracked at all times. After all, that's already the case in school.

Dad, before you even comment: The reason I have a C in biology is that I was out of town and didn't turn in my lab assignment until two days ago.

I'm glad you said something because when I logged on to your school platform today, I was very surprised.

I knew you would be. It doesn't help that my teacher is out of town and hasn't entered homework the past couple of days, either. If you check back on Friday, you'll see the grade go up.

Okay. By the way, I noticed this past week that you've been slipping in Spanish.

I'm on it. Just need to stay after school and meet with my teacher.

The level of frequency and access that Gen Z, and their parents, has had to their performance at school will have a dramatic impact on expectations at work.

If I want to know what is going on with Jonah in school, I simply log on to an app that can lay out for me every homework grade, missing assignment, test score, and cumulative GPA down to the day. It's that customized. I can even pay attention to upcoming assignments and tests.

Gone are the days where a kid could wait by the mailbox a couple of times a year to intercept a report card before their parents got it. Unless the Wi-Fi is down, we parents are constantly in touch with what is assigned and, even more so, with daily progress. Teachers will be the first to tell you that it's a lot of work entering the information into the system. If you fall behind even one day, they have students and parents reaching out for explanations as to why a grade has dipped. It's also a lot of work for parents.

But what happens when Jonah and Gen Z show up at work and this type of customized monitoring is not happening? For some it will be a way to slide by and not be as noticed. Many might feel relief from the stress of constant scrutiny.

However, for most it will feel like something is broken. Not having access to constant custom feedback will be a stressful situation because we won't know where we stand. We will want to pull out our smartphones and get an up-to-the-minute customized report on our progress. The good news is that there have been some exciting advancements in project management software that tracks the steps of a project down to the minute. The key for Gen Z will be to look at these as more than just monitoring whether and when a task is completed, and instead as vehicles for feedback on the job. If nothing else, it is important to embrace these programs because they will give Gen Z comfort in knowing that tasks are being monitored and managers are paying attention.

Sounds exhausting . . . and probably will be, but ask teachers and they will tell you that this level of custom access and frequency is not all bad. It has taught students the value of self-monitoring. Teachers don't have to remind students about deadlines or point out that they are falling behind. The information is available every day. Best of all, students often come to talk to them about it, which has allowed everyone to be proactive and not always reactive.

As a parent, the tools that have been provided to monitor Jonah's school progress have allowed us to truly mentor him and work together. If he is struggling, we all know about it and can talk about it. With workplaces operating at such a fast pace, Gen Z's familiarity with self-monitoring will be helpful to their leaders.

As Jonah mentioned, there have been some big breakthroughs

in technology-based systems that track the progression and completion of projects. However, many workplaces avoid them because they feel they are too complex or provide more detail than needed. That may have been true—until now. The next generation of employees got used to using tech-based programs that gave them custom access and frequent feedback on their performance in high school. The assumption will already be there that similar systems exist at work.

One thing is for sure: We will have to set levels of expectations with Gen Z about how often they can access feedback. Before we complain about Gen Z asking for constant access to it, we have to remember how they've been raised. With or without an app, employers are going to have to figure out how they too can create dynamic report cards that are updated much more often than a couple of times a year.

The more often it is updated, the more customized it will feel to us. Sure, it could be high-tech like the programs used in high school or it could be as low-tech as a quick email, phone call, or drop-by at their cubicle. The good news is that we aren't looking for long, chatty conversations. We want it quick and straight to the point. Our national study found that 67 percent of Gen Z is comfortable with having their manager check in with them but only for five minutes or less.

Finally, besides hyper-custom feedback being more frequent and accessible, it will also need to be broken down, just as Panera figured out for how to train Gen Z. The more managers can think of feedback in sound bites, the more it will feel relevant and even palatable to Gen Z. Broad statements about our performance that spans months and months will be more difficult for Gen Z, especially if the feedback is coming in a formal review months after the work was completed. Gen Z is going to want custom feedback on their performance that breaks down project by project, task by task.

The Echo Chamber

Jonah. Did you read the op-ed piece I forwarded to you?

No.

Why not?

I hate that newspaper!

Why?

I don't agree with what that journalist says. You've sent me her stuff before. She just makes me mad so I don't read her.

That's why I sent it to you.

To make me mad?

No. To make you think.

As I have studied this generation and just how hyper-customized their world is, I've come to have some big concerns as a parent and future employer.

I see how this generation is consuming their news. They can literally custom-pick what source they want to listen to that matches their specific ideals and beliefs. Their entertainment consists of their own ecosystem of sources that they put together. From podcasts to blogs to YouTube channels and more, they can find someone out there who has the exact same point of view as they do. Religion, politics, and even business, they can find sources that actually confirm their beliefs no matter how far-fetched they are.

They live in what many call the echo chamber. The result is that Gen Z might not be as adept at thinking outside their tunnel as we think. Usually it's when we get older that we become more set in our ways, and it's the younger generation that supposedly has the open minds. If all Gen Z hears is ideology that they like or agree with, they will assume they are always right. Even worse, they'll think there is no other point of view to consider.

It's one thing if this causes an intense debate with their parents, but what happens when this shows up with Gen Z at work? Are leaders ready for a generation of employees who might already be set in their ways even though they are brand-new to the job?

As parents and mentors we have to be sure that Gen Z is also hearing what those with different views think and why they think that way. As we all know, there will be plenty of times in their careers where Gen Z will be faced with opposing opinions. Navigating those conversations and situations is critical to their success. If they are only used to being surrounded by their own ideology, when opposing opinions are raised, they will naturally not respond well or know how to respond at all.

This will only lead to the other generations naturally label-

PAULA ABDUL
Singer-Songwriter

Remaining true to yourself and keeping the connection to your heart can be challenging on the road to success. How hard do you think it will be to remain true to yourself and have a successful career?

One-third said it will be very hard to remain true to myself and have a successful career.

One-third said it will be easy or very easy to remain true to myself and have a successful career.

One-third had no opinion.

ing them as bad sports, poor negotiators, or just downright spoiled. We will have to look for tangible ways to help Gen Z get out of their own silos.

Companies and Gen Z can benefit greatly from programs like rotations, where an employee is exposed to all aspects of a company. Job swaps where employees actually switch jobs for a day work great. Environments that foster cross-training or allow shadow days for employees to see what others do within the organization could also be beneficial. The ultimate goal is to help break down Gen Z's tunnel vision.

On one hand, Gen Z has more exposure to the world than any other generation had at their age. On the other hand, a world so customized to what they want . . . can become quite small.

Hyper-Custom Zingers!

- Dig in and get to know Gen Zers' personal brands.
- Personalize the recruiting experience.
- Allow employees to create their own job titles.
- Consider customized job descriptions.
- Personalize career paths to capitalize on employees' ambitions and strengths.
- Create targeted training that combines self-teaching tools with face-to-face mentoring and coaching.
- Incorporate new ways to track, post, monitor, measure, and share performance data.
- Help Gen Z step out of its self-administered "echo chamber" to be exposed to other points of view.

REALISTIC

Jonah, you have one elective next fall. Why don't you take art history?

Why would I?

To learn about art.

Why?

What do you mean, why?

What does that have to do with any of my goals?

Maybe it doesn't but art is part of life. It's something great to know about, whether you go to a museum, or travel to Europe, or someday want to buy some for your house.

Dad, I have a limited number of electives. Why would I take a whole class on art history just in case I buy a painting one day? If I want to know something about an artist or a painting I can always google it.

It's more than just who painted it. You learn all about genres of art, what was happening at that time that inspired artists, fascinating stories about the artists themselves . . .

I think that's great for people going in that direction, but I want to take classes that will actually apply to my future.

When Millennials were at the same age as Gen Z they were filled with nothing but optimism, ready to set the world on fire. They had plans to be the next Mark Zuckerberg or save the planet or even launch the next great start-up. They truly believed they were the generation that was going to make it happen.

The older generations loved their can-do attitude (still do) and would never want to squelch it—especially their idealistic Boomer parents. However, deep down most knew that at some point in Millennials' careers, they might be in for a dose of reality. Usually that wake-up call would be once they had bigger responsibilities than just getting out of bed and showing up for work on time. There's nothing like a mortgage or saving for your kids' college to help you realize that you might not be Mark Zuckerberg and that you don't have time or resources to start the start-up. But for Millennials, believing that it could happen wasn't a bad motivator to get out of bed and try.

Flash forward to my generation and by high school we would be the first to tell you to "get real." The days of teenage dreams to be president or make millions of dollars as a business tycoon have made way for nightmares of not being able to make it at all. Who could blame us? Where Millennials' experienced a time of prosperity and opportunity during their teen years, my generation has grown up in a time of recession, terrorism, violence, volatility, chaos, and uncertainty, to name a few.

As teens, we didn't exactly escape to watch mystical movies such as Harry Potter. My generation was being "entertained" with dark postapocalyptic stories with role models, like Katniss Everdeen from *The Hunger Games*, who face seemingly inescapable scenarios and have to rise above them to create a better society. It's not that we see the world as doom and gloom; it's that we believe if you're going to survive or even thrive, you'd better get real about what it's going to take.

With Gen Z comes a new, more realistic attitude when it comes to careers and getting ahead. Long before showing up at work, it was brewing right at home.

CHRIS ANDERSON
Curator of TED Talks

Do you like the future that you see coming?

Yes: 56 percent
No: 44 percent

For those who do not like the future that they are seeing . . . what aspects of the future will you change?

TOP 3 RESPONSES
Global warming/pollution
Hate and discrimination
Politics

Home Semisweet Home

On one hand it's sort of sad that at a young age when Millennials believed they could own the world, Gen Z is looking at the same world as nothing but fragile. On the other hand, we shouldn't be so surprised, since these same differences played out with their parents.

Idealistic Boomers who believed anything was possible clashed with skeptical Xers who constantly said, "Prove it." Well, now this differential between Boomers and Xers is playing out in their children.

We know Millennials have turned out to be optimistic and often idealistic. But in the case of Gen Z, what happens when skeptical Gen Xers are also raising kids in a complex socioeconomic environment marked by chaos, uncertainty, and volatility? You end up with a generation that at a young age worries.

The J. Walter Thompson agency did a study on teenagers to find out what we are worried about. Sixty-six percent said we are concerned about how our parents are doing financially. This concern was higher than how popular we were in school or how many friends we had. Compare this to Millennial teenagers, who grew up in a better economic time. They were more worried about how many "likes" they had on Facebook. My generation is already worried about the economy.

This goes a lot deeper than simply labeling skeptical Gen X parents as being negative with their kids. Pew Charitable Trusts found that when Gen Z children were young and the recession hit, the median net worth of Gen X parents fell by nearly 45 percent. It's not that Xers wouldn't have wanted to tell their Gen Z children to reach for the stars; it's that they believed the smarter strategy was to keep it real and reach for a paycheck.

Since Gen Z is worried about the future at a younger age, it has changed the landscape of how they even approach high school.

High School 2.0

Dad, I need to go shopping for school clothes.

No problem. Where do you want to go?

I was thinking Men's Wearhouse.

Funny.

No, seriously. The business immersion courses I am taking in the mornings have a dress code that you have to dress as though you were going to work in a professional setting. No jeans, T-shirts, or sweat clothes.

In high school? Every day?

Yup. Isn't that cool? We don't have to wear ties, but I think I want to some days. I have my couple of suits I wear for our speeches, but I was thinking we could get a few pairs of khaki and black pants and a bunch of dress shirts.

I don't even wear that to work.

I know. Otherwise I would be borrowing your clothes.

Who would have ever thought that the workplace would be seeing resumes boasting professional experience as far back as high school? However, a generation that was awoken at an earlier age about the realities of the future is not waiting to prepare for it.

As I mentioned in the Introduction in my elevator pitch, I spend a half of each school day off-campus attending a business immersion program called VANTAGE. This is nothing like the high school my dad had growing up.

Rather than just sit in a classroom studying AP economics or business analytics, I go to an office setting two miles away from my high school and work on projects for companies like General Mills and 3M. These projects provide professional experience in both business and analytics. We still learn the basic principles, but we get to apply them to real-world situations. It's one thing to read a textbook and take a test; it's another to do market research and present findings to business executives while getting the AP credits.

In addition to the professional experience, they help us set up LinkedIn pages, build our first resume, write business plans, and so much more. Hey, it's also pretty cool that I get to be off-campus for the first half of the day and on the way back to the high school stop at Chipotle for lunch. Just saying.

VANTAGE is part of a growing network of schools that started in Overland Park, Kansas, in 2009 at the Blue Valley Center for Advanced Professional Studies (CAPS). Schools such as Jonah's license the program from CAPS and give it their own name.

Corey Mohn, executive director of CAPS, explains: "There is too much pressure on students to focus on test scores and

AP classes, which does not lead to academic engagement. Our goal is to show students how what they are learning applies to their future. We don't focus on a linear curriculum and instead on immersion into real-world scenarios."

On most days, Jonah walks out of the door looking nicer than I do. Even better, on most days, he actually jumps out of bed to get to school . . . or should I say the office.

One thing is for sure: companies partnering with programs like VANTAGE are not complaining. They too want to keep it real and know that they need to get on Gen Z's radar as soon as possible.

UnitedHealth Group (UHG) is a large international health and well-being company. They offer mentors as well as lectures to VANTAGE's health-care track. Pat Keran, senior director of innovation at UHG, said, "These kids are talking about careers at a young age and we want to expose them to potential ones at UHG. We realized that the technology skills that our college students had were developed young. As we dug a little deeper, we realized that high school students would be equally as competent. So if we are going to get the same output in the end, why not get on the radar even sooner?"

If you're Apple or Google, odds are that you are on my generation's radar. But if you are UnitedHealth Group, Deloitte, or 3M, we might not be gazing out the window daydreaming about a career in risk management or food science.

Deloitte has not only realized this, but has added a component that makes their efforts all the more powerful. Their

BILL GEORGE
Senior Fellow, Harvard Business School

What is the biggest dream Gen Zers would like to fulfill in their lifetimes?

TOP 3 RESPONSES
Make a positive difference in the world
Be independently wealthy
Have a healthy, loving family

program is called RightStep. Deloitte professionals volunteer to support public schools in nearly every major market where they have a presence. What makes RightStep different is that it focuses on public schools with students who are underserved minorities. Professionals go to high schools after school hours and mentor students, from help on the ACT to conversations about their futures.

Meredith Fontecchio, senior manager of Deloitte LLP and RightStep Lead, said, "We have over one thousand professionals reaching over six hundred students across the country through one of our signature RightStep programs, Deloitte Academy. Students learn about career paths that they may likely not have heard of, such as accounting, analytics, or consulting. Through our mentoring relationships, we realized that many of the students we serve had not been to an office, so we bring them together in our office and show them what a corporate environment is like. Through this exposure, we can get them thinking about different career paths early on, and simultaneously build a future pipeline."

From funding curriculum to field trips, companies and industries have realized for years that the earlier you catch them, the more likely they are to come knocking on your door. Most have believed that the best thing to do is reach out to college students. However, with Gen Z, companies and industries should reach even further and earlier to high school students. Gen Z is more receptive at a younger age and is taking a realistic approach to seeking out opportunities.

As we mentioned, when you've grown up worrying about the future, there is naturally a push to prepare for it. There is a clear trend with my generation to establish career paths and goals much earlier in life in order to compete later in life. Where Millennials might have been told it's a marathon, not a sprint, and you have your whole life to prepare, my generation feels the pressure. In fact, a study done by Millennial Branding found that 55 percent of high school students feel pressured by their parents to gain early professional experience.

HENRY WINKLER
Actor and Director

Are you aware of your particular gift . . . the reason you were put here on earth?

Yes: 49 percent
No: 51 percent

There are now more than twenty high schools licensing the CAPS program like the one Jonah attends. As Jonah comes home and tells me about his presentation to General Mills or his meeting with his mentor, it's hard not to think that this is too good to be true and doing way more than just preparing him to go to college. In fact, for some participants in the program, this early exposure to the business world is so good that it isn't even worth going to college.

Brady Simmons is a leading-edge Gen Zer who was part of Blue Valley's original program. He explains: "In high school I didn't see a lot of value. It was all about doing enough to pass. So as long as I got a C, I was happy enough. When I joined Blue Valley CAPS I was able to really see a connection between what I was learning and how it applied. It was way more than getting a grade. If I failed a project, I was failing more than myself; I was impacting our project sponsor. I found myself truly loving school."

As all CAPS students who study global business do, Brady wrote a business plan for a potential business. His was designed to help start-ups raise money and then keep investors involved and help grow the business. He believed in his business plan so much that after graduating from high school, he decided to pursue the business while going to college. "After my first semester, I found college to be a lot like high school was for me before finding CAPS. It was all about studying to pass and I didn't see a connection to how what I was learning applied to my life. So I quit college and pursued my business full-time."

One of Brady's first projects was to raise capital for a start-up education technology company. It went so well that two years later, he became an equity partner in the firm. It now gainfully employs sixteen people and has opened satellite offices in four cities. The company continues to grow at a rapid pace with plans to extend the technology beyond the education market into health care and enterprise. The eventual plan is to sell the whole empire and Brady is on track to make that happen. It looks like Brady is doing just fine.

"We are seeing more and more kids like Brady make that connection between what they are learning and how it can apply to their future. Some, like Brady, decide to dive right in," explains Mohn. "In our first five years, we have seen fifteen U.S. patents filed and many LLCs formed. It's not that these kids may never go to college, it's that they don't want to miss their window. If they feel it is in their best interest to leave our program and not go to college to pursue a career opportunity, why should we hold them back? Even worse, why would we ever criticize them?"

It used to be that any experience you tried to get in high school was all about sweetening the resume to help you get into college. Teenagers never really felt they had to think beyond that.

Realistic Gen Z, however, is thinking about preparing for their careers. In fact, our national study found that 84 percent of Gen Z believes that they have the skills necessary to be successful in a professional environment. Gen Z is thinking beyond college to whether or not it is even worth going at all.

Did You Say College or Trade School?

Historically, there has always been one path to success. You graduate from high school and then you go to college, and then you either get a graduate degree or a job. The path hasn't changed for generations or even been challenged, until now.

Our worries about the economy have led to real conversations about what we can and should do to prepare for our futures. One issue on the table is the value of college. More than just our parents' struggles, we have watched how Millennials at such a young age are straddled with so much debt. All we hear about is how expensive college is. Northeastern University found that 67 percent of Gen Zers indicate their top concern is being able to afford college.

Gen Z is more hesitant about going to college or the value of the four-year degree. It might be hard to blame them. More than just hearing about how crippling college debt can be, Gen Z hears from the Bureau of Labor Statistics that one in eight recent college grads are unemployed and that one-half of those employed hold jobs that do not even require college degrees.

For Boomers, a college degree was still the shiniest bullet on the resume and even debt wasn't going to stop them from pushing their Millennial children to graduate from college. What do Gen Z's moms and dads have to say about it? For Gen Xers who have always been more open to alternative routes, debt for a degree might not seem as worth it. So the message they have been giving their Gen Z children is that if you are going to go to college, make every dollar count.

Where college was once a place to explore your future, it is now looked at like trade school, where you go to learn a specific trade. However, this is not how colleges have traditionally positioned themselves. Many have not been ready for this generational shift. In 2014, the beginning phase of the Gen Z college student body, the *Chronicle of Higher Education* reported declining enrollment for the non-elite institutions. More than 98 percent of college presidents said they believe change is necessary and 67 percent said that the change needs to be disruptive. While it's great that they acknowledge things need to change, no one can agree on the best approach to doing it.

Let's be clear. College has tremendous value. However, there does need to be a different value proposition in order to connect with Gen Z.

Previous generations went to college to figure out what they wanted to pursue. I started in pre-med and over four years ended up in sociology and communications, with a brief stint in forensics. It was all about exploring. Compare that to Gen Z, where college is all about implementing a predetermined career.

Two years ago, I dropped off my oldest daughter, Jonah's sister Ellie, at college. She is clear as day that she wants to be an eighth-grade algebra teacher. That is exactly how she picked her university. It has a fast track to accreditation. All along, I have been supportive, but I can't lie: I was also a bit confused. How is she so sure what she wants? When I graduated from high school I thought I wanted to be an obstetrician or James Bond!

My sister Ellie is not alone. In our national survey, 61 percent of

Gen Z said they believe they need to know what career they want before entering college. Why? If we are going to spend the money or go in debt, then there has to be a clear vision as to how what we are learning will literally pay off for us in our careers. Our conversations are less about where you would go to college and more about what you would want to be.

It really is no different from what programs like VANTAGE uncovered in high school. Gen Z wants to see a deep connection between what they are learning and how it applies to their life. Those typical freshman courses, like Art History or American Civilization, while very interesting, are about the past. Gen Z sees the world changing at such a rapid pace. When they pick up a used textbook that smells like moth balls from the university bookstore, it is harder for Gen Z to see how those teachings are relevant to their future.

All that Gen Z hears is how the workplace is looking for practical experience and that the job they may have in later years hasn't been invented yet. Gen Z knows that the ones who get jobs are the ones who have real-life work experience and not necessarily the ones who aced an exam by naming our country's founding fathers. Colleges that can offer real-world experience or draw connections to it are the ones that Gen Z is looking at and willing to pay for.

It's very telling that, according to Northeastern University, 79 percent of Gen Z favor integrating education programs with practical experience such as internships. There is a huge opportunity for businesses and colleges to collaborate more. Beyond just going to college campuses to find summer interns, businesses should be working hand in hand with professors to weave practical experience right into the curriculum. There are wonderful partnerships that are being fueled by both businesses and colleges.

In 2013, Facebook partnered with twenty-two universities to give computer science credits to students for participating in open-source projects. Participating universities include Stanford, Massachusetts Institute of Technology, the University of California, Los Angeles, and Carnegie Mellon, and many more. Facebook engineers worked with computer science professors to build courses that match students with active open-source projects. The collaboration with professors ensures that students get academic credit for their work. Students have worked on MongoDB, Mozilla Open Badges, Ruby on Rails, and Freeseer. The students have proven to be an asset to the project by reducing bugs, and improving efficiency in the open-source projects. Best of all, they can see a connection between what they are learning at school in computer science and how it actually applies and plays out in their careers.

Another great example comes from Maryville University, in St. Louis. Mark Lombardi, president of the university, commented, "We knew that Gen Z would not want curriculum that was developed in a vacuum or that had not been updated for years and years. We looked at our different education strands and then went to leaders in business across an array of professions to help us co-create curriculum. Our students know that they are taking a degree that was designed by faculty and practitioners and that the learning is current."

One of the partnerships, for example, is with Edward Jones for a financial services major. It is truly a win-win. Edward Jones was experiencing a 40 percent drop-out rate among incoming financial service providers, which cost the organization millions. Together Edward Jones and Maryville designed a curriculum so that students would have the necessary skills to be successful in the financial services industry. Partnerships like these are proving to be successful. In fact, 94 percent of Maryville graduates have a job in their chosen field within three months of graduation.

"It's more than just classroom curriculum," explained Lombardi. "You can't just bring in students and have a professor talk at them. Our students are also in professional settings where they see firsthand how and what they are learning applies to the careers they are pursuing."

As for what Gen Z thinks? Maryville has seen a 75 percent increase in enrollment in the last five years since adopting this educational approach of partnering with businesses.

We have heard that at the end of the day, it doesn't even matter where you go to college unless you are going for one of the elite or Ivy League. I can't tell you how many times I have heard my dad and his friends joke about how they have no idea where their employees or coworkers went to college or in some cases if they went at all. However, they do know about each other's work experiences or past places of employment. The message is clear that experience trumps all and are the bullets to try to get on your resume.

As nice as it is that my daughter knows she wants to be an eighth-grade math teacher, I do want her to learn more.

When she came home for winter break, I was blown away by how excited she was to discuss the famous Trojan horse story from her Greek Civilization course. I was feeling so good until she commented, "But don't worry, Dad, I'm also loving my real courses." Shame on me! Clearly I've put too much attention on everything being about practical skills, if she didn't feel this story was part of a "real" education.

Taking poetry, art, physics, anthropology, and more will not only make her a curious person, but yes . . . even a better eighth-grade algebra teacher. In his bestseller *In Defense of a Liberal Education*, Fareed Zakaria argues that the American university experience can create thinkers who can innovate as opposed to skills-based workers who can simply execute. Businesses will not just need Gen Z to execute; they will need them to think and innovate, like Zakaria is talking about. However, this is not what Gen Z hears businesses or their parents talking about.

EARVIN "MAGIC" JOHNSON

Chairman and CEO, Magic Johnson Enterprises

Rank each of the options below in order of importance when choosing a job.

1. Friendly and innovative environment
2. Meaningful work
3. High salary
4. Growth opportunities

It's not that we don't believe in a college degree. In fact, our national study found that for now, 80 percent of Gen Z feel that they need a college degree to be successful. However, we are not a generation that believes it is the only path. It used to be that not going to college was the uncool thing to do. But when we hear that people like Bill Gates, Richard Branson, Larry Ellison, Michael Dell, Ted Turner, Ralph Lauren, Steve Jobs, and Mark Zuckerberg didn't graduate from college, and definitely are not straddled with debt, it's hard not to have an open mind. Also, for a lot of my generation we are seeing some pretty interesting and enticing alternatives.

A case in point is PayPal cofounder Peter Thiel, who started the Thiel Fellowship. This initiative offers $100,000 over two years to forgo college and instead start your own business. The *Wall Street Journal* reported some impressive results of this "keep them out of school" effort, including the fact that "64 Thiel Fellows have started 67 for-profit ventures, raised $55.4 million in angel and venture funding, published two books, created 30 apps, and 135 full-time jobs."

One interesting recipient of the Thiel Fellowship is Dale Stephens, who explained: "My freshman year of college I found myself taking classes like World Religions or World History. Sure they were interesting, but I struggled to see their relevance. There was no context. It seemed it was all about telling me a bunch of facts that happened years ago, now go memorize them."

Dale dropped out and started UnCollege. The idea is to replace the typical freshman year of college and provide context with an education that feels more relevant. The program is one-third of the cost of a freshman year at college. Over the nine month "school year" participants spend three months abroad doing service learning, followed by three months working one-on-one with a mentor teaching life skills needed to be successful, and ending with a three-month hands-on internship program in the real world.

"Participants are usually in one of two camps," explains Stephens. "One would be explorers. These are Gen Zers who don't know what they want to do and need time to explore before they feel comfortable making an investment in college, if at all. The other group would be career finders. These are Gen Zers who are interested in a specific career, but before they make the investment in college, want to understand specific jobs that are available to them and what they would truly be like."

After the program some decide to dive right into an entry-level position in the workforce, and others decide to head off to college. Said Stephens, "We are against the belief that everyone should go to college no matter what. At the same time, we see tremendous value in college once a student has a better connection to why they are going and how it will apply to their future."

One might think that UnCollege threatens colleges. After all, the name implies disruption. However, what Dale has seen happening more and more is that many colleges are now reaching out to partner with him. These colleges are seeing the value in that freshman year providing more context and real-world experience. Dale's vision is that colleges will not just partner with UnCollege, but actually replace their typical freshman year altogether. As he sees it, "Those that decide to go right into the workforce after the first year would likely not have survived in college anyways. And those that do go on to college will be much more likely to not only stay, but also see more value in what they are learning." Considering most other countries have three-year degree programs, this may very well be part of the "disruptive" change the *Chronicle of Higher Education* is referring to.

The Realistic Recruit

Whether it's VANTAGE or UnCollege, there is no denying that Gen Z's realistic attitude will result in resumes the workforce has not seen before. There is also no doubt that their realistic attitude will result in a different mindset altogether, especially compared to Millennials. Because Millennials grew up in more prosperous times combined with a lot of self-esteem; they showed up at work and often felt that the job was lucky to have them. Gen Z, on the other hand, grew up in a recession and had parents with more tough love. As a result, Gen Z will show up and feel they are lucky to have the job.

In our national survey 75 percent of Gen Z said they were more worried about getting a job and starting a career than they were about finding a soul mate.

Because Gen Z feels lucky to get a job, the workplace should not have as difficult a time recruiting or convincing them to take it. This generation might even accept positions for which they are overqualified because that way they can get their foot in the door. As they see it, why waste time waiting to get experiences when you can just get started and hopefully move up? As Jonah said, they have learned that experience trumps all.

For Millennials, it seems all the recruitment conversations were about selling the moon and stars. There were lots of catchphrases like "flex time," "constant movement," and "unparalleled growth."

Now we are seeing a lot of Millennials feeling a bit lost. They spent a lot of money on college and besides being straddled with debt, they are not happy with their careers. Many are even moving home. It seems they bought into a destination and got a little lost along the way. Of course they will figure it out, but watching them go through all of this has an impact on my generation.

The key with my generation will be to not use a lot of big buzzwords. Just be direct and to the point. In our national survey, 85 percent of Gen Z reported that straightforward, constructive communication is most important.

Instead of just explaining the experience we will get, talk to us about what we can learn along the way. Make us Gen Zers feel that we will learn so much we will never want to leave.

At the end of the recruitment day, probably the most important conversation will be around keeping it very real about what the company even does.

Dad, I was doing some research for our upcoming speech to that gravel company.

Nice.

I read their mission statement and couldn't help but roll my eyes.

Why?

They are claiming that they are the foundation for everything in our country because everything that is created starts as a grain of sand.

Well, that probably is true.

C'mon, Dad! You really believe that this company is the foundation of everything in our country today? Please!

Gen Z will want real proof that you can stand behind any claim you make. Mission statements that tell a customer you are changing the world may help sell a product or service. However, over-the-top mission statements probably won't sell a potential Gen Z employee on joining your company.

Are you really changing the world? Because for the record, it's really okay if you aren't. We just want to understand what it is you do and, even more so, why it matters. You don't have to be solving world hunger. Basically, if the mission feels too far-fetched we will find a different mission to sign up for. Ask us why and we will simply tell you to get real.

TOM WILSON
CEO of Allstate Insurance

What is more important to you about a company?

What they sell: 20 percent

Who they are: 80 percent

Real Talk

Boomers in the world of work had to learn an entire dialect of political correctness. Eighty million people navigating the competitive climb to the top wanted to always be fair and constructive. In the 1990s along came Gen X, who felt everyone was spending so much time beating around the bush. Xers shocked Boomers with their straightforward, no-BS communication style. Xers didn't understand why you couldn't just tell someone they sucked and instead had to use phrases like "you have an area of opportunity."

This difference played out in how Boomers and Xers parented. As mentioned, Boomer parents wanted to instill a lot of self-esteem in their Millennial children and focused their conversations on those areas of opportunity. The result was Millennials with delusional goals of being CEO and leaders who were pushed to their limits managing and even tempering Millennials' expectations about getting ahead.

No worries there with my generation. Our Xer parents have been managing those expectations since our first tee-ball game. It's not that mom and dad didn't believe in us; it's that they told us if CEO really is the goal, it's not going to be easy, and besides that, might not be likely to happen at all. We don't feel shot down and in fact we actually feel equipped to get ahead realistically.

This should come as no surprise, but because we are a very realistic generation; we do not like a lot of fluff. Our moms and dads have never sugarcoated the message, and, bottom line, neither should our leaders. Honest communication is what will generate

PAUL POLMAN

CEO of Unilever

What are the values that drive you?

TOP RESPONSE: Family

CLOSE SECOND: Honesty

the most trust with Gen Z. Too many leaders put a lot of stock in their company's reputation as the way to earn trust. However, when you've grown up where some person or organization is getting in trouble every day for being dishonest, reputation alone will not cut it. In fact, our national survey found that only 5 percent of Gen Z said that corporate reputation generates trust. Gen Z doesn't care as much about the past. Number one on the list was "honesty." In other words, if you want to prove to Gen Z that you're the place to invest a career, then keep it real.

However, unlike their Gen X parents, Gen Z will not be as paranoid. When Xers did show up, they always felt that everyone was trying to hide something that they needed to know. That is one of the main reasons why Xers wanted their communication to be so straightforward. If meetings were happening behind closed doors, skeptical Xers assumed the worst. Gen Z, on the other hand, has come of age where it is hard to hide anything. They feel that if there is something they need to know, odds are they will find out. Gen Z does not see a meeting behind closed doors as a threat.

As discussed in the chapter "Mom and Dad," the bond between parents and kids continues to be strong. One thing is for sure: just like Millennials, we don't doubt that when the going gets tough for Gen Z, they too will call their parents. That said, the conversation on the other end of the phone will likely be a lot different than it was with Millennials and their Boomer parents. When Millennials called mom and dad to complain, Boomers not only dropped everything, but also were quick to side with their children, agreeing that the boss was everything from clueless to a moron. When Gen Z reaches out, mom and dad will still be quick to pick up, but they will also tell their kids to suck it up, that their boss is right either way, and that they had best figure out a realistic solution to the situation.

Because conversations with Gen Z have been very real, and because they witnessed the Great Recession during their formative years, Gen Z is not clueless when it comes to the realities of their careers. They know that it is going to be tough. They also know that they will have to be willing—and they are—to roll up their sleeves a little further than we have seen in a long time.

Paying Your Dues: Making a Modern Comeback

When Millennials showed up at work, Xers and even their Boomer parents were taken aback by how much they had to manage their expectations. It's not that having big aspirations to reach for the top of the ladder was a bad thing; it's that no

CHRISTIANE AMANPOUR

Chief International Correspondent, CNN

Do you regard employment or professional life as an entitlement or are you prepared to start at the bottom of the ladder and painstakingly work your way up?

76 percent said they are willing to start at the bottom and of the ladder and painstakingly work their way up.

14 percent said they regarded employment or professional life as an entitlement.

one took the time to explain to Millennials that they wouldn't be promoted to vice president after six months on the job.

Gen Zers feel lucky to have a job and are indeed willing to start at the bottom rung and work our way up. We know that we will have to put in effort and prove ourselves in order to get ahead. In fact, our national survey found that 76 percent are willing to start at the bottom. We will pay our dues provided that leaders are very specific about what paying dues means. It can't be broad, like "work hard." As we saw in the "Hyper-Custom" chapter, what we pay in dues will have to be as specific as possible.

If only there were more Traditionalists in the workplace to see that the notion of dues paying is actually going to make a fashionable comeback. However, it is still different from Traditionalists' concept of dues paying, which was more about putting in time. The idea that advancement is based on tenure alone is still dead. Telling Gen Z that they will be eligible to be promoted after one year will not make sense.

Competitive Boomers loved to brag in front of the boss on Monday morning that they were in the office over the weekend. This will not be the case with competitive Gen Zers. Those who pay real dues will not be the ones putting in the most time, but rather the ones who figure out how to get the job done most efficiently. Gen Z will live loud and proud that there is a fine line between working hard and working smart.

Goodbye, Life Stage; Hello, Life Phase

So many leaders complained that Millennials always seemed to have one foot out the door. These leaders were constantly worried about retention. For Gen Z, all those real dinnertime conversations about the recession left them not just in search of security, but with a desire to plant both feet in one place.

In our national survey, 61 percent of Gen Z said they would stay at a company for more than ten years. Of the 61 percent, 31 percent said they would be willing to stay more than twenty years! Of course, there are many factors at play here, but this is not something we have even seen on the table for a while.

When I shared this statistic with my Traditionalist grandfather, he was speechless with joy. He couldn't believe my generation would actually want to spend a lifetime at one place of employment. This from a guy who has worked as a doctor at the same hospital for fifty-three years.

I did have to tell him not to get too excited and that odds are, most Gen Zers will not be at a job with the same company for fifty-three years. I also had to explain that there is a big difference between staying a lifetime and a long time.

Traditionalists and Boomers came of age where the longer you stayed with an employer the better your resume looked. Nothing said loyalty more than one place of employment. Along came Xers, who in the late 1980s saw those same people kicked to the curb as the economy took a nosedive. Xers also saw the end of what was known as a "job contract." From the get-go, Gen Xers were not willing to pay the same price for success.

Thus was born the label of "job hopper," for a practice that carried right on over to Millennials. In their case, they often hopped to a new job because the only way to move up was to move out. For Millennials, staying at a job often meant losing money. So of course older generations might be caught off guard to hear that Gen Z is willing to stay at a job for ten-plus years. The difference is that we still shouldn't expect Gen Zers to only have one place of employment on their resume.

One of the fascinating fruits of being a very realistic generation is their realization that they will live a lot longer than the rest of us. A lifetime to Gen Z is a lot different than a lifetime to previous generations. According to demographer Professor James Vaupel and his co-researchers, 50 percent of babies born in the U.S. in 2007 have a life expectancy of 104 or more. For Gen Z longevity is definitely part of the equation. They know they will likely be working for years and years and years.

Partly because they will have to. Partly because they will want to. And partly because they will feel good enough to.

The switch we are seeing is that Gen Z doesn't think in life stages like the rest of us did, where you go to college, get a job, get married, have kids, retire, etc. Gen Z thinks in life phases where these events (or stages) could happen more than once in a life and likely will. They could start their careers in a phase of working hard at climbing a corporate ladder for fifteen years, getting loads of experience. Then they could enter the childrearing phase and work for ten years at a smaller company that offers more flexibility so they can be around more with the kids. Paying for their kids' college could then have them entering a phase of throwing their hat in the start-up ring for another ten years. Come their empty-nest phase, they will still feel as though they have a good twenty-five or more years left in them and could try an international stint, go back

HARVEY MACKAY

Author of *Swim with the Sharks Without Being Eaten Alive*

Is there an age where you will retire and stop working or do you anticipate always working in a chosen field?

50 percent said they want to work in a chosen field until they are unable to do so.

25 percent will retire in their sixties.

25 percent had other varied opinions.

DARA KHOSROWSHAHI
CEO of Expedia

What are the top three reasons you would stay at a company for more than five years?

TOP 3 RESPONSES
Pay/Salary
Friends/coworkers/environment
Pleasure in the job

to a big company, maybe even school. For Gen Z to say that they will stay at a company for ten years seems very doable, if not normal. Again, it may seem like a long time . . . but to Gen Z, it's definitely not a lifetime.

Jonah, let's stay an extra day when we are in Tucson for the speech and visit U of A. We really should start creating a list of what you are looking for in a college. I found with Ellie that going to see some is the best start.

I guess.

Why not?

I've been thinking, Dad. Maybe I don't need to go to college. I am getting such great experience doing Gen Z work for organizations. And let's face it, I am making some good money, too.

Who said you can't do both at the same time?

That's true.

And what if you decide that you don't want to do this someday?

Oh, Dad . . . I highly doubt I will be speaking about Gen Z for the rest of my life.

Then don't you think you should get an education?

But I am getting an education. In fact, a really great one. Think about all the companies I get to research and how many executives I get to meet. If someday I decide to move on from Gen Z, I'll have a great network.

But there are so many other things you can learn at college that will make you all the more successful.

Like what?

Classes in how to be a great entrepreneur.

They have those?

Some colleges do. If you want to keep it real, then let's make that the first item on your wish list.

Realistic Zingers!

- Help Gen Zers have realistic conversations about careers and college.
- Expose Gen Z to careers in realistic ways at younger ages—aim for high school and even middle school.
- Explore public/private partnerships between educational institutions and employers.
- Accept that college isn't the answer for everyone—explore what other avenues can equip Gen Z to have productive lives and careers.
- Encourage thinking and innovation along with more pragmatic educational pursuits.
- Create career paths focused on skill building rather than just title or rank.
- Reflect realistic messages in recruiting.
- Be honest about work hours and rules.

WECONOMISTS

By the way, didn't you say these guys couldn't afford our speaking fee so we had to discount it?

Yes. But remember, there are great prospects in the audience so it is still a great opportunity.

Uh, Dad . . . filet mignon, fancy vegetables, some kind of fluffy potatoes. Not to mention those people in tuxes playing the violin in the corner. They don't seem to be too strained for cash.

Speakers and training are out of one budget and the food and entertainment is out of a different budget.

That makes no sense! If you ask me, getting good speakers and trainers is way more important than making sure my asparagus is tied together with some green leafy thing.

I agree, but for as long as I have been speaking, it's just the way it is.

Why wouldn't the training people just ask the food people to cut back on something so that they can pay for a speaker? If you ask me, they could do without the violins. Just pipe in some music from your iPad. No one will know the difference.

One of the biggest movements in the world today is what has been called the "sharing economy." It's the notion of people sharing their goods and services with each other and coordinating through community-based online platforms. Millennials were the generation who really launched the movement. From a room in your house to a seat in your car to a tool in your shed, they were creative in seeing a way to tap into excess capacity and monetize it.

Gen Z has never known a world without the sharing economy.

Ever since I could hold a smartphone, I have had some type of app I could click on to share or optimize resources. Why buy a bike when someone close to your house can let you use one? There's an app for that called Liquid. Should all the neighbors really be paying for Wi-Fi when we could be sharing it together? There's an app for that called Fon. I love helping to plan our family vacation and clicking on Airbnb to see if there are any luxury apartments, with an ocean view, of course, that we can rent. And how about the ultimate? Uber!

For Gen X parents who grew up haunted by missing children staring them in the face from milk cartons over breakfast, it would have been hard to imagine hopping into a stranger's car and driving away. However, to Gen Z it makes all the sense in the world.

Getting into a "stranger's" car doesn't seem weird to me at all. I am on GPS and can easily be located. Not to mention the app has the phone number and license plate of the driver. The same goes for the name and address of a stranger's home. Doesn't seem scary at all. Of course, I'm not saying that bad things never happen, but those things can happen just as easily in a hotel or taxi.

As mentioned, Gen Z has never known a world without the sharing economy. That said, they became old enough to really join in after many of the original kinks had been ironed out.

Idealism Made Way for Realism

Millennials helped launch the sharing economy. They took their collaborative nature and combined it with the tech world. They learned from books like *The Rise of Collaborative Consumption* that 80 percent of the items people own are used less than once a month. Therefore, it was pretty simple . . . we don't all need to own the same things; it is better for the environment if we share.

And thus a new industry was born. Companies like Ecomodo, Share Some Sugar, and Thingloop popped up to offer you the ability to share anything from tools to toys or borrow a cup of sugar. As great as the value proposition sounded to help save our planet, within five years they were all closed. So, what happened? There was only so much that people were willing to do.

Let's say I am putting together my new desk and need a drill. So I click on the app and connect with someone five miles away.

Then we have to communicate back and forth a few times to figure out the best time for me to come get the drill. Then I have to drive there to get it. I come back and assemble my desk. Now I have to get back in touch to coordinate a time to give back the drill. I then have to drive back and drop it off. I could not think of anything more inconvenient. I would rather just buy a drill.

Sharing economy companies that seem to be lasting, such as Uber and Airbnb, are more focused on convenience and value, as well as our carbon footprint. Say goodbye to idealistic sharers and hello to the new generation of weconomists.

Gen Z is all about a sharing economy as long as it is about being convenient, efficient, and economical, too.

Wesourceful

Okay . . . just want to say that I think we are we are probably taking the play on "we" too far, but my dad likes the word *wesourceful*. Anyway, after watching the world rebound from everything from stock market to job market crashes, as well as Millennials saddled with so much debt, Gen Z has seen the need to be resourceful.

In the opening story to this chapter, it seemed only natural, if not smart, to me that the speaking budget be shared with the food and entertainment budget. As we look to bring the sharing economy to the office, we will show up and think that if we are sharing bathrooms with the business down the hall, maybe we can share Wi-Fi or a printer? If we are all going to the same trade show, perhaps we can share transportation or, even better, a booth! That's convenient, efficient, economical . . . and thinking like a weconomist.

This mindset will go beyond just looking for ways to be resourceful with funds to looking for ways to be resourceful with skills. When Traditionalists came of age at work, they had a great model for getting things done: you simply delegated as much as you could to your secretary and then you did the rest. From an expense report to a lunch reservation to preparing for a presentation, if it could be handed off, it was. It's not that secretaries were less important; in fact they were very important. It's that they were better at those skills and more cost-effective. Plain and simple.

Over the years, we all got computers and, bit by bit, many of those tasks secretaries would do landed back in our laps. After all, there were software programs that would help you do an expense report or make a reservation, and copy machines were now small enough to sit right on your desk or credenza. You didn't need someone else to do it for you.

We have trudged along doing these things ourselves and now Gen Z will enter the workplace and will likely raise their hands and ask . . .

Is that really the most convenient, efficient, or economical?

Gen Z will boomerang back to an efficiency model that Traditionalists embraced. No, they will not expect to have personal secretaries, but they will believe in leveraging the collective.

Let's say I'm in sales and have to write a proposal, but I'm just not a great writer. I can get it done, but it will take me a while and a lot of stress. It would make more sense to me to find someone who is a better writer than I am and ask him or her to do it. It will not only get done better and a lot faster, but will be less stressful as well. That's thinking like a weconomist.

Imagine this: Jonah's boss walks into his office and asks him about a proposal. He replies, "Since writing isn't exactly my forte, I asked Mason to do it. Not sure if you have seen any of his proposals, but they are killer. He said he'd have a draft by end of day. I want to go over it before sending it to you. Is it okay if I get it to you tomorrow morning?"

It is hard to imagine that Jonah would hear "Great job!" In fact, he would likely be told that he isn't doing his job.

There will be a lot of generational issues at play here. Boomers, Xers, and even Millennials will be thinking, "I had to write proposals, why shouldn't you?"

For Traditionalists and Boomers, handing off tasks was often based on tenure and paying dues. The higher you climbed the ladder, the more you could push tasks down. This was a privilege earned by seniority, not available to the new recruit.

Gen Z will walk in the door with the weconomist mentality and believe that delegating to people like Mason is not just part of our job, but is being smart about it. It will have nothing to do with tenure. If we have no problem clicking on the app TaskRabbit and getting someone to do an errand for us, why wouldn't we find someone at work who might be better at something than we are?

It's a mistake to assume that once I ask Mason for help, I'm sitting back with my feet up. I could be a wiz at doing expense reports, which Mason is always behind on. We will simply trade. He does my proposal and I do his expense reports. It's not about feeling as though you're too good to do a task or unwilling to pay dues. It's that you're not good at them so you find someone else who is. That's thinking like a weconomist since it comes back to convenience, efficiency, and being economical.

A concern is that if we let Gen Z delegate all tasks that they aren't good at, they could likely plateau. Part of coming of age in the world of work is developing new skills. It will be important to let Gen Z know that we need to be efficient with our time, but that we are also willing to invest some time . . . especially in them. It might take Jonah longer to write a proposal, but with some solid training, it could be a wonderful investment to make. Jonah could become really good at it. Or not. Most important, Gen Z will have to know that investing in skill development is not being inefficient.

Leaders will also have to decide if at the end of the day they want to control who does the job or just that it gets done right. Could Gen Z's approach create an environment where work does get done better and faster? If so, as mentioned in "Hyper-Custom," we will have to focus less on job descriptions and more on skill sets.

For Gen Z, being resourceful will be about sharing talents at all times regardless of what your job or position is. Let's say that a department needs a coordinator to help them organize their annual trade show booth. They know the exact skills they need. In our world, they simply log on to an app to get the help.

This same mentality should apply at work. Couldn't someone or even a couple of people with the necessary skills in a different department help out even if it means they don't change jobs?

Couldn't their skill sets be shared? I know the first thought will be, "What about your regular job?" And who will pay for this?

As we will discuss in the "FOMO" chapter, we operate best when we can switch between tasks often. The work will still get done. Let us prove that to you. Why couldn't we have internal postings for skills instead of just jobs? What if there were a database of skills? You need someone who is good at logistics? Click on "L." Expense reports? "E." You get the idea. One thing is for sure: There are so many skills and talents that employees have that we don't tap into, because we often don't know about them. We only ask about the skills needed to do the job they are hired for.

This level of wesourcefulness could be a wonderful thing internally, but what happens when Gen Z starts leveraging the collective good with more than just their coworkers?

Can't We All Just Share?

Dad! I'm so excited. I found us a great trademark attorney who can help us really assess if we have something worth trademarking or if it isn't worth it.

Great! Who is it?

One of the guys from the law firm we are speaking at next month.

Our client? What did you say to him?

I just told him that we weren't sure if what we had was worth trademarking.

But you did tell him that it is still based in primary research and solid case studies . . . right?

Uh . . . we didn't really talk about that.

Jonah! I don't want them thinking we are showing up next month with something we just made up.

Dad! Relax. He was cool and said I could send him what we've got and he will take a look at it for free.

In my eyes, this made perfect sense. I had connected with the attorney in preparation for the speech only to uncover he specialized in intellectual property. We were already connecting, so why not ask him? My dad did not agree. We've gotten into a few of these arguments.

We recently had a local client from a university that is located on the other side of town. She asked for some copies of my dad's books, so my dad asked if I would make the drive and drop them off. In my conversations with her, I remembered her saying she lived in our neck of the woods. When I talked with her, I asked her if she wanted to swing by on her way home. Made sense to me. She was already on the road and going to drive by. However, when she knocked on the door and I gave them to her, let's just say my dad was clearly not happy. I personally think it was because he was in his sweaty gym clothes, but he said it wasn't.

Okay, I won't deny that I wasn't thrilled to be standing on the landing all sweaty when she briefly walked in, but it was more than that. I felt I was teaching him a lesson in customer service. From my point of view, you don't make your client drive to your house. You drive to where they are. Jonah felt he was teaching me how to become a weconomist. He thought I was being wasteful as he explained, "Why drive all the way across town and waste my time and gas?" In some respects, it was hard to argue with him.

The lesson for all of us is that Gen Z will truly take the concept of "we" to new places when it comes to getting any job done. Asking a vendor for something isn't new or that difficult. After all, we are already paying them something and deep down we know that they will have a hard time saying no. Who doesn't take advantage of that once in a while? But asking a client? Let's go back to the intellectual property attorney. In my eyes, a new client is one of the last people I would ask for something from—especially for free. Odds are, a Boomer would be right there with me. The fear is that we would be exposing a need when the goal is to always look as buttoned up as possible.

As Gen Z sees it, that isn't very realistic, since all businesses have needs. Some of the best relationships will be with your clients, so why not leverage the collective good with them as well? We won't see it as exposing a need or looking less capable; we will see it as being convenient, efficient, and definitely being economical. In other words, thinking like a weconomist. Keep in mind, leveraging can go both ways with a client. It won't always have to be about asking the client for something . . . It can be about giving something, too.

Jonah, where were you?

I was at Heidi Ross's office.

Did she ask for more books?

No. She was telling me when she stopped by how annoyed she

was because she couldn't figure out how to use Slack at her office and all of her employees are on it. She gets teased for not being as tech savvy and didn't want to ask the other employees for help. I offered to get her all set up and so I drove over after school.

That was nice of you.

It took me ten minutes to set up. It was no big deal. She must have thanked me a hundred times.

This idea of loaning your skill set to someone outside of the office reminded me of a very cool program when Traditionalists started to retire. They had spent their whole life working with the ultimate goal that one day you just stopped. However, when that day came, for many it felt more abrupt than they had imagined. They missed being busy and the community they had been with for so many years. Most of all, they missed having a purpose. Companies knew that they had to get new talent in the door and up to speed. A win-win was a phased retirement. Rather than be at the office five days a week, a Traditionalist would be around two or three. The threat of brain drain could be avoided by having the retiree still around to answer a question or two. Slowly the newcomer learned the job and the Traditionalist got used to not showing up at the job. Here's the cool part: The days that the retiree was not in the office, they were "loaned" to nonprofits that needed their help. Traditionalists had the wisdom and experience that so many nonprofits needed and often couldn't afford.

When my dad told me about this, my immediate response was, why don't they do that with all generations and not just those retiring? Especially mine! My dad talked earlier about me learning how to provide better customer service to clients. Why not loan any special skills we have to help our clients? If my generation can bring something to the table at work, likely in technology, surely it could be useful to clients. Having us out of the office to share our skills and provide better value to clients may cost the company something, but what we would get in return would be worth it. Now that's thinking like a weconomist!

Me to We

Leveraging the collective good as employees is just one part of Gen Z's weconomist mindset. The whole other side is their role as philanthropists. Like the previous generation, Gen Z is excited about how they can make the world a better place as well as how they can partner with their employers in doing so. However, they will surely go about it in new ways.

We did not coin the term *weconomist*. One of our dear

ARNE DUNCAN
Former U.S. Secretary of Education

What are you planning to do to change the world?

TOP 3 RESPONSES
Volunteer in the local community
Become more involved in social causes
Start my own business

friends, the world-renowned philanthropist Craig Kielburger, did. Craig has built a global movement on the notion of millions of youth going from Me to We. Craig's organization, WE, has been a part of our lives both personally and professionally. After selling my company, I went to work for his nonprofit to pioneer the movement across the United States for five years. It was some of the most rewarding work of my career as I witnessed firsthand hundreds upon hundreds of Gen Zers engaged in philanthropic activities way beyond anything I ever saw as a kid. This immersion and exposure to Gen Z is one of the main reasons I wanted to go on and pioneer the dialogue with Jonah. Craig's story began when he was just twelve years old. He read an article in the newspaper about a boy named Iqbal who had been sold into child slavery. Craig was the same age as Iqbal and couldn't believe that such a horrible thing could take place in the world. A fire was ignited. Craig went to his seventh-grade English class with the newspaper article and asked who wanted to help. Eleven kids raised their hands and his movement began. One of the first things this group of kids did was call a well-known international human rights organization. When they explained that they wanted to help, the comment on the other end of the phone was, "Sure! Do you know where your parents keep their credit card?"

The person couldn't even imagine that a group of twelve-year-olds could make an impact. Craig commented, "At that time, the two most uncool things to do were glee clubs or social justice clubs. I was pushed into many lockers. However, this didn't deter me from believing that the younger generation could indeed make a difference. I was determined to make it cool to care."

And that he has done. That one club of twelve-year-olds that started in Craig's basement has turned into 2.3 million young people across Canada, the United States, and United Kingdom, all committing to take action on service projects they are passionate about both locally and globally. Craig's WE movement has shown that you are never too young to roll up your sleeves and do what you can to make the world a better place.

Let's be clear: There are an endless number of amazing nonprofits engaging with youth today, but this one we feel is unique because it is not promoting a specific cause but rather motivating a generation to engage in any of them. WE is about creating our next generation of philanthropists.

Every day at school I learn about some activity that I could get involved in that involves helping the community. I can sign up to tutor inner-city youth, volunteer at a food bank, attend a talk about clean water programs overseas; the list literally does go on and on.

STEVE BALLMER

Former CEO of Microsoft, Owner of the Los Angeles Clippers

What fires you up? What's your passion?

TOP RESPONSE: Help people/make people happy

It's just assumed that you and your friends are doing some type of community service.

Sure, wanting to round out your resume for college applications drives some of it, but as we see it, that's okay . . . it's still a win-win and doesn't make it any less authentic. However, there are many other reasons why Gen Z rolls up their sleeves to help out. We can thank our parents, who have instilled in us not just the importance of giving back, but that it is truly our responsibility to do so. We also don't have to be told that the world needs our help. Rather than learn third-hand that bad things are happening in the world, we see them beamed to our phones 24/7. We see videos of people running from buildings that terrorists have attacked, people starving to death, natural disasters wiping out communities. According to Unilever Project Sunlight, 78 percent of Gen Z are concerned about world hunger, 77 percent are concerned about children around the world dying of preventable disease, and 76 percent are concerned about man's impact on the planet. It's all right before our eyes. In fact, it's all right at our fingertips.

With the advent of Facebook, it was the Millennials who were first to tap into social networks and use technology to do good. By the time Gen Z was old enough to help out, we weren't even on Facebook and instead had even more tools at our disposal. We learned from Millennials not to take our connectedness for granted and to use it to change the world.

Like we saw happen with the Millennials, there is no denying that giving back is just part of Gen Z's DNA. And with Gen Z this desire to give back will show up at work in new ways.

Meaning and Money

During Millennials' formative years, they saw intense events get closer and closer and closer to home. Columbine, the Oklahoma City bombing, and 9/11 did more than scare them; it instilled a passion to make the world a better place. On top of that, they had Boomer parents who were often burned out and said to their children, "Look, if you're going to work as hard as I have, then you should really do something you care about."

Combined, the two forces resulted in a generation that when it came time to launch their careers put meaning at a premium. It's not that Boomers or Xers didn't want meaning in their lives; it's that they hadn't looked to their jobs as the main vehicle. Millennials caused a big shift in the workplace. Suddenly companies were revamping their recruiting techniques to pitch the opportunity to make a difference even more than make a living. Boomers and Xers were not used to explaining to someone whose role it was to answer a phone how they were changing the world. For them, the model had always been that you enter the workforce and over time ascend into roles that are more meaningful.

Meaning was enough for the Millennials, or at least for a while. In recent years, since the onset of the Great Recession, many have realized that perhaps it isn't enough. In addition, for many entry-level jobs, the idea that they were changing the world was more of a stretch. As hard as leaders tried to paint a save-the-world picture, they were still just answering phones. It's not that Millennials have given up on their role to make the world a better place; it's that they have been forced to broaden their search for meaning beyond work.

So what's shifting again for Gen Z?

Like the Millennials, we will want to make a difference as well as work for companies that are having an impact. In fact, in our national survey, 93 percent of Gen Z said that a company's impact on society affects their decision to work there.

We are also going to want to have a say in where charitable dollars are spent. I think it is so cool that companies like Wells Fargo are choosing to put the power of giving in the hands of their employees by partnering with a nonprofit called DoTopia. They are moving from their traditional United Way campaign model to a donor-directed approach by opening up Personal Giving Accounts for their employees. Managers award their employees with DoDollars in these accounts, which they can then donate to the charity of their choice.

However, as much as a company's impact on society may affect our decision to work there, it won't necessarily be enough to convince us, as it was for Millennials. Our Gen X parents want us to be good citizens and give back, but they have made no bones about the fact that charity will have to start at home.

The recession has led us to be more realistic and not as idealistic as Millennials were when they were starting out. Sure, we will want to hear about the difference a company can make, but part of being a weconomist means we will want to still talk about salary first. Our national study found that 77 percent of Gen Z puts pay at

DAVE GILBOA
Founder, CEO of Warby Parker

What are the most important factors to choosing an employer for Gen Z?

TOP RESPONSE: High salary

FOUR OTHER RESPONSES THAT WERE TIED:
Opportunity to develop my skills
Great relationships with coworkers
Flexible working environment
Caring, empathetic leaders

the top of the list. Meaning is not the new money with us. A stable job and paycheck is.

And don't even try to convince realistic Gen Zers that by answering the phones, we are lighting the world on fire. A switchboard maybe, but not the world.

The weconomist attitude has Gen Z looking at giving back through a more businesslike lens. What we hear from Gen Z is that if a company does good business first, that will yield more profit for them, which can then move the needle on causes. Simply put, if companies make more money, there will be more to give back. Perhaps Gen Z is more idealistic than they realize. It hasn't always been proven that the more you have the more you give.

Hopefully Gen Z will fight that battle and encourage successful companies that they need to give back more.

Time Is Still Money

Dad. Did you hear about Mr. Owens building that house?

Yes, it was for Habitat for Humanity.

His son Eli said he and his coworkers missed weeks of work to build it.

Isn't that cool that his job offers volunteer opportunities like this?

I guess so.

What do you mean you guess so?

Dad, let's face it. Mr. Owens isn't exactly the handiest guy. Can you see him building anything?

Well, no. But that's not really the point.

What is?

His company wants to give back and is loaning its employees to help out.

I get that. But hear me out. Think about how much more productive Mr. Owens would be if he spent those weeks helping to raise money instead of learning how to hold a hammer. He could probably raise enough to build a few houses; they could then hire real builders to get it done in a fraction of the time.

Do me a favor . . . don't say that to Eli.

Millennials valued workplaces that didn't just offer volunteer opportunities but organized them as well. Gen Z will also love workplaces that tee up opportunities to give back. As they enter the world of full-time employment, they too will miss having the free time to volunteer, especially given how prevalent it has been since grade school. However, wearing their weconomist hat they will also be saying, let's be savvy when it comes to the power of "we." Maybe not all nonprofits just need volunteers. Gen Z will reinvent the notion of being a volunteer. They will look to help causes do good business or raise money in creative ways. They know that at the end of the day, profits are what nonprofits need most in order to make a difference.

If For-Profit and Nonprofit Had a Baby

Companies learned fast that one of the best ways to pull in a Millennial customer was to connect the purchase of any product or service to a cause. It became commonplace to go shopping and be told that thanks to your purchase something good was going to happen. Brands worked hard at identifying what their cause would be so that they could put it to work for the brand, and of course someone else in need. Buying some Cheerios? You're also helping childhood literacy. Picking up some Yoplait? You also help with breast cancer. Need some Pampers? While you're at it, you're helping with vaccines. Out of nowhere, cause marketing became enough of a movement that entire firms were launched. However, the market has been flooded to the point where it is almost assumed your purchase has a feel-good twist.

Along come Gen Z weconomists, who will now push it even further.

One of the coolest parts to Craig Kielburger's international nonprofit WE is that it also has a sister for-profit organization called Me to We, which sells a variety of socially conscious goods. For example, jewelry that is beaded by hundreds of Kenyan women is sold in stores like PacSun and Nordstrom. One-half of the profits from Me to We (for profit) go to WE (nonprofit). WE is able to operate at a nonprofit-industry-low admin rate of 10 percent. The ultimate goal is that Me to We will generate enough profit to cover any administrative costs so that 100 percent of all donations made to WE can go directly to its causes. As Jonah would say, now that's thinking like a weconomist.

I can buy a beaded chain from Me to We and help provide a source of income to African communities. I can buy a pair of glasses from Warby Parker and have another pair donated. Shoes? I can go to TOMS. Backpack? There's State Bags. This is how my generation has learned to look at giving back. We don't necessarily see for-profits and nonprofits as being at opposite ends of the spectrum. We see them coming together and believe that every transaction can accomplish something good.

For Gen Z, our formative years have seen the rise of social entrepreneurs like Craig. There are a variety of definitions of "social enterprenuer," but the one we like best is rather simple: "using business to solve social issues." Millennials saw the birth of this movement and thanks to their voice on social media they really let the world know. For Millennials, the giveback was almost enough. It's not that they didn't care about the product they were buying; it's that they cared even more about the impact of their purchase.

As social entrepreneurialism has grown, the quality of the product has become as important as the impact the purchase is making. Just doing good isn't enough. Again, we assume most products are doing good these days.

Scot Tatelman, cofounder of State Bags, commented, "When we started State Bags, we put the mission front and center. For every backpack sold, a backpack is hand-delivered to an American child in need. During the first year we realized that people don't care about the mission if the product isn't cool and isn't priced right. We repositioned. The focus is on the usefulness and design of our bags and the mission is the cherry on top, but not the main focus."

The intersection of for-profit and nonprofit is the type of mindset that Gen Z will push for as they enter the workforce. Companies will not be able to reinvent themselves overnight, but Gen Z weconomists will push for marketing and company foundations or community relations departments to sit at the table together and even invite product development to join the meeting.

Employee Versus Philanthropist

As nice as it will be to have these weconomists as employees, it could be dangerous for our future philanthropists. Gen Z's focus on convenience, efficiency, and being economical might not always play out the same way in philanthropy.

As a parent, it's awesome to see your children excited about

GOLDIE HAWN

Actress

How do you define empathy and is it important to you?

69 percent said empathy is important or very important.
12 percent said empathy is not important.

How do you define empathy?

TOP RESPONSE: Feeling for others

helping to make the world a better place and even have fun doing it.

I remember how exciting it was when my friend Ryan nominated me to do the ice bucket challenge to benefit ALS research. It was not only fun to make the video and nominate others, but there was no denying it was thrilling to feel a part of the crusade against a horrible disease. Every day I logged on to see videos of people doing the ice bucket challenge. It was great!

While it's nice to watch your kid give back, it was a bit disturbing when I asked Jonah six months later what happened with the ice bucket challenge. He didn't have a clue about what was going on with ALS other than knowing that they had raised "a lot of money." Most disturbing was that he and his friends didn't seem to care.

We will have to mentor Gen Z and teach them that championing causes takes time and needs more than just a one-

and-done. Sure, we need to make giving fun and exciting, but it can't always be that way. Causes cannot afford for this future donor and volunteer base to feel like they have been there and done that. They can't be "over it" before the causes themselves are. Though wanting things to be more convenient, efficient, and economical is thinking like a weconomist, it doesn't always make for the most strategic philanthropist.

Weconomists Zingers!

- Recognize Gen Z's focus on optimizing resources via the sharing economy but doing it efficiently.
- Be prepared for them to adopt "skill sharing" in the workplace.
- Stay open to blurring the lines between employees, clients, customers, and vendors as excess capacity is shared.
- Expect Gen Z weconomists to help companies do good by doing well.
- Help Gen Z focus on real results, not just feel-good gestures.

FOMO

Jonah, what are you doing?

What do you mean?

You keep swiping your phone screen.

Oh. My biology test is supposed to be in the grade book, so I'm just refreshing it.

Every thirty seconds?

Yeah, it's supposed to be in by the end of the night.

It's 6 p.m. and there's a lot of time left in the night. Why don't you relax and do something else. How about checking every hour or even half hour?

What's the big deal?

What years ago would have been written off as youthful impatience is now much deeper and in many ways serious. It is a trait that defines Gen Z and what many would even call a syndrome.

FOMO: Fear of Missing Out.

From the latest news around the world to who asked whom to the prom, Gen Z is always in the know. It's not that surprising considering they are thumbing their way across as many as five screens at once. From a TV, to laptop, to desktop, to tablet, and of course mobile phone, any bit of information is always literally a click away.

This access is obviously available to all generations and not just Gen Z, but other generations still remember a time when it wasn't just a click away. Traditionalists, Boomers, Xers, and even Millennials recall waiting for updates that came much less frequently. Other generations definitely have liked the improvement and access, but haven't always been dependent on it like Gen Z is.

My generation just doesn't know a world in which one isn't connected at all times or doesn't have constant access to any information. Being connected to information and our peers is like breathing air to us. If we don't feel connected we feel as though something is wrong. Sparks & Honey reports that Gen Zers spend 41 percent of their time outside of school with computers of one kind or another, compared to 22 percent just ten years ago, as mentioned in the "Phigital" chapter. Where Millennials could be described as digital pioneers, Gen Zers are digital natives.

Like Jonah said, being connected is like breathing to Gen Z. A study by J. Walter Thompson found that Gen Z valued their

Internet connection more than going to the movies, getting an allowance from their parents, attending a sporting event, or having cable TV.

With constant access comes constant exposure to everyone and everything around you. At all times, Gen Z knows what everyone is doing. They know that if they unplug, the world just keeps on going and at a fast pace. This only leads to a feeling of having to stay on top of everything at all times, which becomes more and more impossible to do.

We can't sign off because everyone is always signed on. I can be part of a group text and put down my phone to go work out. When I come back thirty minutes later, I have missed out on a whole conversation, not to mention all the other ones that I am involved in or at least following. Something that was big news when you woke up is already miles of scrolling down your feed and by lunchtime isn't just ancient, but lost. The problem is that

TINA WELLS

CEO and Founder of Buzz Marketing Group, Author of *Chasing Youth Culture and Getting It Right*

In a world full of technology, how do you achieve balance in your life?

TOP 3 RESPONSES

Spending time with friends
Spending time outdoors
Taking time away from technology

you always feel like you have to check. You don't want to be the one who missed out on what everyone else is talking about.

Our fear of missing out has us constantly checking in. Our national study found that 44 percent of Gen Z checks in on social media at least hourly, with 7 percent checking in more often than every fifteen minutes. Interestingly, 1 in 5 Gen Zers spends more time refreshing their Twitter feed than even reading it.

Two of my favorite findings from our study are that 1 in 10 Gen Zers would rather go three days without refreshing their underwear than go three days without refreshing their Twitter feed and 32 percent would rather go three days without a shower than go a week without their phone. Now that's FOMO!

There are only two places you can go to these days where cell phones are actually forbidden: places of worship and movie theaters. However, even a movie isn't going to be sacred. The AMC theater chain is considering allowing the use of cell phones. In a *Variety* article, CEO Adam Aron explained: "When you tell a 22-year-old to turn off their phone, don't ruin the movie, they hear 'please cut off your left arm above the elbow.'"

You know it's gotten intense when Pew Research reports that 91 percent of Gen Z say they have their digital devices in bed. However, before the rest of us shake a finger at them, today 65 percent of all people who have smartphones sleep with them on or near their beds. For the record, that's just shy of the number of married couples who sleep together. That's scary.

We've all heard the phrase "keeping up with the Joneses,"

the idea of comparing your accomplishments and material possessions to your neighbors. The phrase was popularized in 1913 when a comic strip called *Keeping Up with the Joneses* was created by cartoonist Arthur R. "Pop" Momand. So in essence, a fear of missing out has been around a long time. Just ask any Traditionalist housewife how she felt when her neighbor three doors down got the new Hoover 800 vacuum cleaner or a Boomer when all the stores were sold out of Pet Rocks.

For the other generations, they were only exposed to what others had when they saw each other face-to-face. The circle of family or friends was also a lot smaller. With Gen Z, their exposure to others is truly global and at all times they can see what their network of hundreds, if not thousands, have. They don't have to wait to bump into them face-to-face. It's right there on their smartphone.

The other truly notable difference is that with other generations, the fear was based more on missing out on having an item, or as the definition says, material good. Gen Z is seeing not only items that others have, but experiences. For previous generations to know that someone else went on a trip, ate at a restaurant, saw a concert, got a job, met a celebrity, went to a party and so on, they would likely have had to see that person or hear about it in a face-to-face conversation. For Gen Z, experiences are beyond easy to share. As a result, our next generation of workers will always be distracted and tempted not just by what others have but also by what they are doing.

Let me give an example. I just looked at my feed and can see that my friend Tucker just landed in Mexico, Zach is at the hockey game, Will is at a bonfire with six other friends of mine who also posted pictures, Anna and Bella scored tickets to Justin Bieber, Joey signed up for the ACT test, Reece is playing golf, Miles and Ben are on the lake, Courtney got into college, Thomas is at the gym, Sadie and Ellie are at the dog park, Zoe passed her driver's test, Jacob is going to the Vikings game, Scotty got a new car, Ryan is happy about Burger King's new chicken nuggets, Morgan is with Ryan at Burger King, Tucker made it through customs in Mexico . . . at least that's what's happening the last three to five minutes. Other than going to the Bieber concert and taking the ACT test, it all sounds great to me. How could I not feel like I'm missing out?

The Never-Ending Bucket List

Let's face it, it is not just Gen Z. All of us are seeing the daily feeds from our own personal networks. Everyone is likely suf-

ROBERT GREENBLATT
Chairman, NBC Entertainment

Because Generation Z is so connected to their devices, are you missing out on experiences that might better you for the workplace?

Yes: 52 percent
No: 48 percent

fering from FOMO these days. It used to be if you wanted to catch up on what your old high school friends were doing, you waited until the next reunion. Now you just log on. However, there is a difference when you are older and more set in your life compared to Gen Z, who are just trying to find themselves. There is also a difference between the haves and have-nots. While Jonah can feel he is missing out on a Vikings game or a trip to Mexico, at least these things are within reach. For those who can barely afford the data plan on their phone that is broadcasting the feeds, they not only fear falling behind, they fear being left behind.

There are a lot of side effects from FOMO that as parents we have to watch out for. It's more than just feeling like you are missing out. We have to be sensitive to the emotional toll that FOMO has on Gen Z. They are growing up in a world that constantly fuels jealousy, feelings of being left out or of inadequacy. It can get so bad that fear becomes anxiety. This leads to sleep deprivation, depression, and constantly being reminded of their shortcomings.

Also, since everything is just posted at the same time, there are no filters. One minute you could be hearing about chicken nuggets; the next you could hear about a death in the family. Gen Z will need help prioritizing what things they are truly missing out on and what things really don't matter.

It isn't just parents who need to be dialed in to the side effects of FOMO. What about bosses? What exactly happens when FOMO shows up at work?

Can I Have Your Attention, Please?

With more and more stimulus coming at Gen Z, their ability to focus has become a hot topic. Of course, everyone believes that the younger you are, the less able you are to focus. This is likely true, but research does show that Gen Z's attention span is shorter than previous generations' was at their age. Gen Z has on average an eight-second attention span, which is down from twelve seconds in 2000. According to the Centers for Disease Control and Prevention, 11 percent of children 4–17 have been diagnosed with ADHD. This is up from 7.8 percent in 2003.

Teachers have been dealing with this, watching Gen Zers sit in school desks long before employers will be watching them sit in cubicles. Pew Research found that 87 percent of teachers felt that technologies are creating an "easily distracted generation with short attention spans" and 64 percent felt that today's digital technologies "do more to distract students than to help them academically."

A lot of this does come back to FOMO and is already showing up in the workplace. At Old Navy the majority of their workforce is Gen Z. In fact, over the next five years, they expect to hire at least 100,000 Gen Zers. For years, they had a policy that, while on the sales floor, employees had to leave their cell phones in the break room. When it was time for a break, employees could check their phones. Seemed simple and obvious, but it wasn't.

They noticed that Gen Z employees had a harder time focusing on the job because they felt so disconnected and that they might be missing out on something they really needed to know. Rather than fight it, Old Navy actually changed their policy and now allow employees to have their phones on the sales floor with them.

Some may say that the company gave in or gave up, but according to Leslie Anderson, senior director and head of field HR for Old Navy, the truth is the complete opposite. "Gen Z still knows that working with a customer comes first. If even having their phones in their pocket allows them to be more present for a customer, then it is worth it. We realize that this is who our workforce is and we need to try and accommodate. We want to continue to explore and find new ways to engage our Gen Z employees, get them excited about our brand, while providing great customer service. However, our goal is to not just make this about our Gen Z employees, but about our stores as well."

Smart employers will need to redefine "attention" and help employees deal with the distractions that are now available to them.

Multi-Taskers vs. Task Switchers

Every parent of Gen Z comments on how one minute—I mean second—Gen Zers are talking on their phones, the next they are texting, then they're on the computer, and so on. Because Gen Z has almost a frantic pace for staying on top of so many things, most just assume they are amazing multitaskers. The natural response would be to pile it on for them. What manager wouldn't get excited about that directive?

The wake-up call is that in actuality, Gen Zers are not good at multitasking. Their brains are not focused on a lot of things at one time. What they excel at is task-switching, where they can go from one task to another seamlessly and frequently.

This is key for leaders who can't just give them one or two big assignments that might take a long time. Gen Zers will need coaching on how to break assignments down into more palatable tasks that they can ideally move between. Keep in mind that they have an eight-second attention span. That's not to say they can't learn to sit for longer; still, that's not how they are wired.

Marketers have had to manage this when trying to get Gen Z to pay attention to their messages. Even a sixty-second television spot is eternity to a generation that is growing up with videos that are no longer than six seconds.

We need to go from task to task to task as quickly and as frequently as possible. It comes back to FOMO. We've been "trained" to believe that the more we can touch, the less chance we are missing out on something else.

Career Path(ssss)

When it comes to career paths, all the generations have had some level of fear that they could be missing out. For Boomers, there was one path: up a ladder, and with each rung a fancier title and bump in pay. Any fear they had was because they knew there were fewer rungs the higher you went and the goal was to see how high you could make it.

At some point, you would settle into a rung as high up as you could get. When Xers came along they really shook things up because they weren't as caught up in a competitive climb to the top or what rung of the ladder they were on or their exact title. Any fear Xers had came from their skeptical sense that at any time the ladder could come crashing down.

Their mojo involved constantly getting bullets on the resume so that if something bad were to happen, they would be able to land on their feet somewhere else. Xers embraced things like lateral moves, which Boomers saw as the kiss of death.

In a Boomer's eyes, a lateral move meant you were stepping aside for someone else to pass you in the race and climb to the top. However, in Xers' eyes, a lateral move meant you were going somewhere else to learn a whole new set of skills, which only added more employment-friendly bullets to the resume. Then came the Millennials, who felt that if they were going to spend the majority of their days in a job, they'd better be making the world a better place. For them, meaning was the new money, and they were afraid they would end up in a job that wasn't making a difference somewhere for someone.

So now comes Gen Z and our greatest career fear will always be that we are missing out on something else that might be better. Once again, the workplace will be rocked, since Gen Z will likely want to pursue multiple paths at the same time. Our national study found that 75 percent of Gen Z would be interested in a situation in which they could have multiple roles within one place of employment.

If you constantly fear that you are missing out, it is hard to imagine putting in months and months in just one position in hopes that you may move up. It's also very hard to imagine doing just one thing when you see everyone around you doing so many cool things. My generation imagines a scenario where we can do multiple jobs at one company. Is it such a stretch that I find a job at a company where I work with the PR or marketing team for part of my day to tap into my journalism passion, and sales or training another part of the day, since I love public speaking?

Pressure will be on to keep careers exciting and Gen Zers less fearful that they might be missing out on something. Think task-switching. It makes sense considering that the more you are doing, the less chance you will miss out on opportunities.

So many large companies are primed to attract Gen Z because they can offer such a vast array of opportunities. However, many will miss the mark because they are still stuck in silos. It may just be that smaller companies will have an easier time with Gen Z. It's not unusual for a smaller company to pitch thus: "Around here you get to wear a lot of hats because we are smaller. We need everyone to be able to do lots of different things. We aren't like the big guys that have tons of departments with lots of people just doing one job."

Granted, multiple jobs within one company might be too much for companies to implement for Gen Z. However, at a minimum, managers will need to offer Gen Z multiple projects to be tackling and switching between. The more these projects can be across different lines of business or functions, the less chance Gen Z will feel they are missing out. Managers need to keep Gen Z up to speed on how their project integrates with all the other efforts being made in the company.

Companies that have embraced rotation programs will hit a home run with Gen Z recruits. For example, Boeing offers two-year rotational programs in business, engineering, HR, and IT. Throughout the two years, new hires are exposed to a variety of business functions and have access to mentors and leaders across silos. Each part of the rotation offers new learning and development opportunities, new networking opportunities, and hands-on work experience. Rotation participants are also able to travel to different offices. From Southern California to Puget Sound to Oklahoma City, these Boeing recruits have an opportunity to explore many paths. It would be hard to feel as though you were missing out on anything when you get to see and experience so much.

Then there are companies that aren't even getting hung up on what jobs employees have at all. They are simply hiring them and putting them to work on different projects. When one project is over, the employee can move on to the next.

KATIE COURIC
Journalist

How committed are you to sticking around a company if your roles continue to grow?

73 percent said they are very or extremely committed to sticking around a company if their roles continue to grow.

Ideally, at some point, these employees find a more permanent position. As much as this caters to Gen Z wanting to see and do a lot to avoid FOMO, it is actually helping these companies with some FOMO of their own. They know a person is a great fit but they may not have an exact position in mind. They still know that there is a lot to do. Why fear missing out on a good employee when they see one? Just bring them in and get them started.

Intuit and Facebook, for example, are making offers to recruits without having a particular job description. Instead of looking for specific jobs or even expertise, these employers are on the hunt to uncover "transferable talents," such as problem-solving or analytical abilities. Marcus Buckingham, a consultant who has advised Facebook on employee evaluations, says, "Companies are realizing they should recruit for innate abilities or attitudes rather than skills applicable to a specific job."

Is *Bored* Even a Word Anymore?

Most Xers and Boomers can remember saying to their parents, "I'm bored," only to have them respond with, "Go outside and play." Along came Millennials, whose parents were proactive to get ahead of their kids being bored. One thing was for sure: It wasn't as easy to just send your kids outside to play. The fear of them ending up on a milk carton was a real thing.

Boomer parents did a brilliant job of not only avoiding boredom, but exposing their Millennial kids to so many great opportunities. From sports to music to language immersion,

Millennials were one programmed generation. Lots has been said about it leaning toward overprogramming, but it's hard to criticize a generation of parents who have truly worked so hard to enrich their kids' lives.

Gen X has followed suit and has also worked hard to expose their Gen Z kids to an array of activities. One difference, however, is that there is a little less pressure on helping them avoid boredom because technology has stepped in as the best babysitter of all. Boomer parents heard Millennials ask the famous question "Are we there yet?" on many long car rides. Gen X? Not so much. In fact, thanks to the iPad and a set of headphones, the parents aren't hearing much at all. As soon as Gen Z knew how to zoom, pinch, click, or swipe, they knew how to stay entertained.

As long as the power doesn't go out, we are good to go. We can always thumb through our social media feeds to pass the time, but even better, there are hours and hours of endless videos for us to watch on YouTube. We can easily stay entertained while sitting around on the coach, in the waiting room at the dentist office, in the bathroom, or even at school.

What concerns developmental psychologists about Gen Z showing up at work is that they have grown up in a world where being bored is not something they have ever had to tolerate. Most generations can recall many a day where being bored on the job was just part of the job. From a half-day meeting to a longer-term project, sometimes work is just boring.

This will be shocking to Gen Z. It will be even more troubling that if they are bored on a project, they will not have the luxury of simply "clicking" out of it and going to something else like YouTube. It's not that Gen Z can't work on boring projects. We all have to. It's more that there's a difference between projects that are truly boring and those that just take a lot longer, with more deep thinking.

The longer projects will be harder for Gen Z, who will want managers' help in getting creative to avoid being bored. It might be as easy as changing up where the work gets done physically. Sitting in the same office working on the same project can get easier if you can switch it up and shack it up at a coffee shop, where at least the music is better. Or it may be more complex, like readjusting timelines so that the project can be broken up into chunks, allowing Gen Z to task-switch a little.

Of course, no one likes to be bored, but there is still a difference. Other generations have dealt with it, compared to Gen Z, who grew up believing that boredom is not something you need to ever endure. It's not that managers will have to plan out every hour of every day for Gen Z; it's that they will need to be sure that there is variety. They won't be looking to take a break and do nothing, either. Sounds great to the rest of us, but remember, downtime doing nothing would only create more fear with Gen Z that they were missing out on valuable time doing something else. A great gift managers could give to Gen Z is teaching them how to deal with downtime. Embrace Google or 3M's approach, which is to give employees time to just think and create. Again, this will not come naturally to Gen Z.

Hire a Creeper

I don't think we should look at FOMO as always being a bad thing. As my dad mentioned, our fear of missing out has us constantly checking our feeds. But what if we put that to work in the office? If my generation is that concerned with what is going on in our social lives, you can bet we will be just as concerned with what is going on in our professional lives. We will not want to work for a company that is falling behind or missing out on something. Gen Z will be sure a company is not missing out on any latest news about the competition or things going on in the industry. I think that will be a great thing we bring to work.

It's a good point. As we all know, one of the biggest downfalls in a leader is when they become too internally focused or are wearing blinders. Gen Z can be the eyes and ears for their employers on the competition.

Okay, Dad, I checked out that other Gen Z speaker and they don't really have their own data.

Did you see him speak?

No. I creeped on his social media sites.

I'm not sure I want to know what that means. I assume it's legal.

Dad, relax! I went to his LinkedIn page and looked through all of his posts. A lot of them are articles from the media that he likes. He has written about eight blogs; however, whenever he includes a stat, it's from someone else's research. He even quoted ours. His Twitter feed is pretty lame as he just retweets anything that is generational. He retweeted more than fourteen of our tweets. I will say, though, his writing is pretty funny. Oh, I forgot to mention that he doesn't have a YouTube channel and is only listed on two speaker's bureaus websites, with Gen Z as one of three topics he covers. His fee is cheaper than ours. He seems to do a lot of speaking in the finance industry for some reason. I need to look more into that.

Wow. How long did that take you?

I did it in biology. They were showing a movie. I didn't have a ton of time, but it's a start.

To get this level of information years ago would have taken hiring a private investigator or someone going undercover. Obviously today this information is available to all of us, but why not let a Gen Zer stay on top of it, since it is second nature to them? From the price of stocks to the latest marketing campaigns, Gen Z will want to stay on top of it all. How can that be a bad thing?

Fad Versus Trend

We will need to teach Gen Z to differentiate between a fad and a true trend. A fad comes and goes quickly and a trend has more longevity. A fad is more shallow, where a trend is more deep.

Most businesses will not be able to afford to take action on something that is more of a fad. By the time a business even pulled together a meeting to discuss something, we would have to be sure it wasn't old news.

Gen Z's staying on top of so much information has not allowed them to really go deep into any of it. It's one thing to know that Tucker is in Mexico; it's another to truly know all the ins and outs of his trip. Is he having a great time, how long is he there, is his whole family with him, what's the food like, what's the Mexican culture like, and so on. For Jonah to try to know that, he would miss out on Reece playing golf, Miles and Ben's time on the lake, Cole's new car, and of course Ryan's elation over his Burger King chicken nuggets.

As mentioned, Gen Z will be perfect for the role of staying on top of the competition and various industry information. However, Gen Z will have to understand that one post might not mean more than . . . well, one post. They will need to learn to monitor and look for multiple posts that they can share with their coworkers and managers and thus together identify a true trend.

Just Go for It!

I will echo what Jonah mentioned earlier. FOMO isn't always a bad thing.

One of my favorite findings in our national study was that Gen Z was not scared of failing, but was more concerned with not getting to try at all.

Part of understanding the effects of FOMO is realizing that we will always be up to trying anything. Our fear of not getting to do what we see so many others around us do far outweighs trying something and then failing at it.

The fact that Gen Z is not as scared to fail should not be overlooked. This has not necessarily been the case with previous generations, who have been way more cautious from fear of failure. If you were a Boomer and competing with 80 million others in a climb to the top, one wrong move could have you out of the race. There were just too many others around you who were excelling.

Gen Xers were already loaded with so many negative stereotypes from challenging the way things had always been done that failure would only fuel the perception that Gen Xers could never make it.

Failing with Millennials has been interesting in that they have often not been allowed to fail. If you got eighth place, you didn't lose or fail. In fact, you still got a trophy. Boomer parents' quest to build their Millennial children's self-esteem had them paying most, if not all, attention to where Millennials excelled. As we discussed in "Hyper-Custom," when Millennials showed up at work, oftentimes their first employee review was the first time they heard some not-so-great feedback. Managers were suddenly reaching for a box of Kleenex. In a national study we did for our book on Millennials, less than 5 percent of those in other generations felt that Millennials were equipped to handle feedback.

Gen Z is ready for good and bad news. We aren't scared of failing or bad news because we have had parents that have allowed us to fail and even taught us how to. One of the biggest lessons from my dad comes from our being at my snowboard competitions together. When I win, it's okay to be happy, but he always reminds me that someone else around me has lost and to keep it cool. Make no bones about it, we do the victory dance back at the condo.

Even more important, he has taught me that when I do lose, the first thing I am to do is walk over to the winner and shake his hand. When you're a teenager, this is not easy, but I know this will serve me well as I go on to compete in the real world.

One of the greatest assets to starting a business with Jonah has been his passion to push for new, innovative approaches. He just wants to go for it and doesn't worry about failing at all. For example, after years of asking audiences to turn off their cell phones before a presentation, Jonah designed an interactive app that has them using their smartphones throughout. It does trivia, live polling, uploads custom resources and links. I will be the first to admit it is cool, but I am also cautious. I hope it is not a distraction and that it actually enhances the presentation.

Cautious? That's an understatement. Every time I have wanted to test it with an audience, he tells me that it's not the right one, they're too conservative, it's not ready, and so on. The way I see it, if it crashes in the middle of a presentation, then we tell them to put their phones away. He's had years of doing that.

In my eyes, if it crashes in the middle of a presentation, then that is likely to be one of the main things they remember. It would be no different than the time I spilled water on my mic during a speech and not only blew a fuse, but caused sparks. Weeks of preparing and all the audience remembers is how the podium almost caught on fire. We've had the same conversation over and over.

Okay, Dad, the app is up and running. We can use it for our speech next Monday.

Shouldn't we test it a few times?

That's what we are doing next Monday.

Jonah, I don't know if I want to test an app with an audience of over four hundred people.

But Dad, the whole idea is to stay on the cutting edge and push audience interaction to a new level. If we don't do it, someone else will for sure. It's only a matter of time. I think it's important for our reputation.

I hear you. But the whole idea is to train the audience on Gen Z and what makes them unique. If they get all frustrated logging on and using the app because it's glitchy, then we lose them.

But if it's glitchy, then we can learn why and make it even better. Besides, we're teaching them to think like Gen Z!

Other generations have always been concerned about what others would think if something wasn't perfect or, even worse, if it tanked. Because they don't fear failing, Gen Z will be less worried about perfecting.

There is already an undercurrent with my generation that if you haven't tried and failed at a few start-ups, then you're doing something wrong. The stigma for Gen Z is not associated with failure but with the lack of experimentation. For my generation, it is more important to start and experience than it is to be perfect at something.

If companies do not have a robust research and development department, Gen Z will be here to start one. The upside is that they embrace what many are calling MVP—minimal viable product. They will keep teams from overthinking things and instead focus on going for it and learning from it.

The downside, however, is that managers will have to make sure that the fear of missing out on something else doesn't lead to shortcutting the task at hand.

We ran into this before we even built the app.

I actually know some guys at my school who are programming wizards who can make it for us. I'll talk to them about it and see when they can get started.

Hold on! Before we even talk to them about it, there is a lot we need to do. We should first look at other apps that might already be out there. Maybe we should find a consultant who has created apps like this. I want to get our head around the budget. Oh, it's also a good idea to talk with some of our clients and get their opinion.

But Dad, we—

Let me finish! We will need to talk with meeting planners to see what technological obstacles we might have with audiences. One thing is for sure: We should build a prototype first and test it.

Are you finished yet? Great, by the time you're done, Gen Z will be retired and it won't matter.

You Think of It . . . Then You Make It

Historically, when anything new is created within an organization, it goes through a very linear and often thorough process. It is usually something along the lines of you think of it, you design it, you send it to review committees, you budget for it, you do a prototype, you test the proof of concept, you redesign it, send it back to review committees, tweak the budget, prototype again, test again, send it into production.

For Gen Z, it really is about MVP. In our eyes, there are really only two steps to innovation. You think of it, and then you make it. Gen Z will be confused why innovation has to take so long and be so drawn out. FOMO will have us wanting to get it done and out there.

All I wanted to do was create a simple app that we could use for our speeches and you would swear my dad was creating the new Facebook. I was so excited to create it and within five seconds he made it sound so boring. I couldn't help but think that his approach was risky because it would take too long and waste resources we didn't need.

The ironic part was that I couldn't help but think that Jonah's approach was risky. We had to meet in the middle and it wasn't easy. I was not about to just let some programmers start building something based on an idea. At the same time, Jonah was able to show me how we could get there faster and even more cost-effectively by eliminating a lot of the steps.

There is a fine line between minimal viable product and risky shortcuts. According to Pew Research, 68 percent of teachers think that digital tools make Gen Z students more likely to take shortcuts. There will always be certain standards that need to be met and communicating them constantly to Gen Z will be critical to success.

FOMO = Frequency

Speaking of communicating with Gen Z, just as their trait of being realistic asks managers to keep it real, not to sugarcoat, and not to beat around the bush, FOMO will have some requirements of its own.

Where being realistic requires transparency, FOMO requires frequency.

If we are refreshing our feeds hourly, at a minimum, I can only imagine how quarterly updates will fly with my generation. Remember, 40 percent of Gen Z in our national survey said that working Wi-Fi was more important to them than working bathrooms. So clearly we are putting a premium on staying connected, which is an open invitation to sharing information with us all the time.

Where the workplace for years has been thinking in quarters, they are thinking in minutes. What happened in Q1 will not nearly be as important as what happened before lunch. Their fear of missing out will be too great to ask them to wait for information of any kind. It's simple: Share company information as often as you can.

This applies not just to information related to the companies they work for, but even more so, to feedback and information on the employee's own performance.

All the generations have pushed for change when it comes to feedback and information. As mentioned in "Hyper-Custom," Gen Z's parents, the Xers, challenged Boomers for more frequent feedback. The once-a-year review was not enough. Xers fought hard and many companies instituted semiannual reviews, which was a big deal.

The motive for Gen X was rooted in their skepticism. Without feedback, they assumed the worst. Collaborative Millennials wanted it more often, but their focus was on making sure everyone weighed in. Why just get my boss's input, when there are managers, coworkers, customers, and more who see me work every day? Companies reacted with more and more 360-degree feedback systems.

So now comes Gen Z, who, like the Xers, will want feedback frequently and, like the Millennials, will want it from a lot of different sources. However, with Gen Z feedback will be taken to a whole new level.

The challenge is that my generation is already quite used to a feedback system that works for us. In fact, we get feedback on things we are doing every single day and multiple times a day. It's simple: We post something on our social feeds and within seconds can see what people think based on how many likes we get. Even better, how many comments people make and what they are saying.

How will even a semiannual feedback system ever work?

They will need their own feedback feed where they can see if what they are doing gets likes or not and if anyone has any comments. However, it will have to be more authentic than some coworkers sucking up and just hitting a "like" button!

Will It Ever Be Good Enough?

Gen Z's FOMO will be an asset in the sales and marketing department. In fact, good sales and marketing professionals have been tapping into FOMO for years. You'd better bet when the gentleman knocked on the door in 1957 to sell the Hoover 800, he was quick to tell Mrs. Jones that Mrs. Smith had just bought one. Mrs. Jones couldn't order one soon enough, since nothing would be more traumatic than everyone showing up for bridge the following week and she still only having the Hoover 650, which did not have the headlamp.

Gen Z's FOMO will help sales and marketing since they will know exactly how to make potential buyers fear that they might be missing out on something big and that they had better buy if they want to stay on the cutting edge. Deploying FOMO will help make a potential customer feel as though what they already have will never be good enough.

That's all fine if you are contemplating whether or not you need a new vacuum cleaner. But what about when you are contemplating bigger things, like your life?

A big concern with FOMO and my generation is that by constantly seeing that friends have things you don't or experiences you aren't having, you can end up feeling as though everything could always be better. It's almost like self-punishment. For every post that you make sharing something that you have or are doing, there are hundreds of others going up at the same time showing all the other things you are missing out on.

To make it more intense, after you do post something, you wait to see if others even care. Tucker might be feeling great about his day and post an epic picture of the Mexican sunset, but when it only gets 67 likes compared to Zach's post about scoring the winning goal at the hockey game, which gets 117 likes, Tucker might actually feel as though he was the one who missed out on something. Even a trip to Mexico can feel as though it's not good enough.

FOMO can form unrealistic expectations about how life should really be and this could be a serious threat in the workplace. As excited as we may be that Gen Z says they are open to staying at a company longer, if they are constantly seeing everyone around them land new jobs and experiences, will they ever feel content long enough to even consider staying? They will always be tempted. When they see a friend or even a friend of a friend get a new job that looks pretty enticing, it will be not only tempting but oh so easy to reach out and ask about it. It's just a click away and without even realizing it, they are "applying" for a new job.

It will be crucial to take the time and point out to Gen Z what they are learning and how it is unique. Ultimately we want them not to have any fears that they are missing out. However, keep a listening ear and encourage them to share with you what they do feel they are missing. Ideally you can help. If not, they might just leave . . . but even then, smart

FOMO Zingers!

- Understand how intensely Gen Z experiences FOMO.
- With employees, expect to redefine what it means to capture their attention. Find ways to help them deal with distractions.
- Help employees break down big projects into manageable tasks, then check in to make sure they are focused properly.
- Remind employees what they are learning, how they fit into the larger picture, and the achievements they've had to help combat career FOMO.
- Put Gen Z's "creeping" skills to work for you.
- Specify whether you are okay with a quick survey of available information or need them to take a deeper, more thoughtful dive.
- Tap into Gen Z's risk-taking capabilities.
- Help them define "good enough."

companies leave the door open. Many Gen Zers might find that the grass is not any greener. If they do return, they will be all the more committed and can be your best signal to the rest that they should not fear they are missing out on anything!

DIY

I don't need a tutor!

Jonah, you really think you're going to learn how to take the ACT better by watching YouTube videos?

Why not?

It's not that easy. You need a proper tutor.

Dad, they have hundreds of ACT videos on YouTube.

I just don't think it's worth risking it.

What am I risking?

Not getting a great score.

Look . . . if Julius Yego can learn how to throw a javelin by watching YouTube videos and go on to win the world championships, I can pick up some tips for the ACT and do just fine. I don't need a tutor.

■ ■ ■

Gen Z is truly the do-it-yourself generation.

World champion athletes like Julius Yego from Kenya—who is not only self-taught, but whose *only* coach was YouTube videos—have raised the bar for what it means to do it yourself. For the rest of us, the DIY concept was geared more to the odd fixer-upper home endeavor or maybe an arts and crafts project. For Gen Z, they look at everything, even their careers, through the lens of doing it themselves.

The Democratization of Information

If you grew up with the ability to log on to YouTube and learn how to do anything from tile a bathroom to speak Swahili, wouldn't you believe you were capable of doing anything yourself?

It's more than just the ability to source information online that has instilled Gen Z's DIY trait. It started with watching their own Gen X parents. Xers didn't trust institutions to do things for them. After seeing so many institutions fail or be called into question during their own formative years, Xers believed that the smartest thing to do was to never rely on someone else. So when it came to parenting, the tone was set for Gen Z that often the best thing to do is DIY.

Our Gen X parents have told us that we don't have to follow traditional paths. They didn't just give this lip service, either. We grew up watching Gen X challenge the status quo. Take education. It wasn't so unusual to meet someone on your baseball team whom you didn't recognize. You figured they must be homeschooled. It was no big deal. The National Center for Education Statistics reports that between 2003 and 2012, the number of homeschooled American children rose 62 percent.

More than just watching our parents embrace DIY during our formative years, we have truly seen the end of the middleman as we know it. With the push for automation and apps that do everything from make a reservation to find a job, Gen Z doesn't know a world where you would ask a travel agent to help you plan a trip. Our world has been about DIY. Especially as we have entered our college years.

While many may balk at an online degree, Northeastern University found that more than 50 percent of Gen Z believes an online degree would be regarded in the workforce the same way as a traditional degree is. In our eyes, an online degree allows us to do it ourselves. Sparks & Honey found that 75 percent of Gen Z say there are other ways of getting a good education than going to college. It's not that we don't value education; it's that the doors have been opened to DIY.

So what happens when DIY shows up at work?

Going Rogue

The good news is that an independent, self-reliant DIY bunch does sound great in a fast-changing world. The bad news is that in the world of work, where Millennials have pushed for team building and collaboration to become cornerstones, this attitude may not be so great.

In one corner we will have Millennials who have taken collaboration to a new level. They know there is no "I" in team and naturally band and work together. Millennials have always believed that two heads are better than one. And in an ideal situation, why not have a dozen heads? Millennials not only harness what everyone brings to the table, but also celebrate what they can accomplish as a team.

In the other corner, we have 42 percent of Gen Z saying they would rather finish a project on their own and get special recognition than finish the project with a group and everyone receives credit. It is very telling that our national survey also found that 71 percent said they believe the phrase "if you want it done right, then do it yourself!"

Millennials will likely feel offended when DIY Gen Z shows up and doesn't immediately join in for a round of kumbaya. As we said, it was really no different for their Boomer parents when Xers came into the workplace.

Tackling this dynamic between Millennials and Gen Z will be one of the most important first steps. Will the 71 percent of Gen Z who believe that "if you want it done right, then do it yourself" know what "doing it right" even means? Gen Z is so used to figuring out everything on their own that they will assume their definition of a project is the right one and just go with it.

We can't afford for Millennials to be so turned off that they simply turn away. If we check in with Gen Z too far down the line, we run the risk of too much time and even resources being wasted.

In busy times, we could very easily get used to Gen Z going

off on their own to get things done. In fact, we will likely come to appreciate it much like Boomers did with Gen Xers. However, that took time. Millennials will need to get very savvy in doing handoffs to Gen Z. They will need to set expectations around what a project entails.

Even more important, Millennials will have to set ground rules for how and when check-ins will work. This will require them to take off their own generational lens and realize that a lot of collaborative team meetings won't be as effective for the DIY generation. Twenty percent of Gen Zers in our national survey said they would rather go to the dentist than have their boss check in on them frequently.

Source It Yourself

Gen Z's DIY attitude means they will push organizations to bring a lot of functions in-house that have traditionally been outsourced.

Whenever I bring this up to companies that we speak to, the first thing I hear is that the reason they go out of house is that they don't have the resources in-house. My response is to ask them if they really know whether they have the resources in-house. We've mentioned this throughout the book, but Gen Z will push companies to uncover more skills within employees that have been hidden because they weren't part of a job description.

Gen Z innately knows that these skills exist but many employers are blind to them. Joan from accounting who is up late watching YouTube videos might just have more to offer than spreadsheets.

She has a knack for graphic design and could be the one to design the holiday card instead of going out of house. Maybe Brian from marketing is a wiz at carpentry and can save the company a dollar or two and over the weekend fix the employee lounge. I think it's so cool that at Google, 55 percent of courses are taught by employees of all ranks who have been identified with unique skills and talents—many of which are not part of their job. Topics range from engineering-specific courses to even, yes, fire-breathing.

Managing DIY Gen Z will involve embracing their push to identify internal skills that could actually save time and money. At the same time, part of mentoring DIY Gen Z will be showing them how to analyze the fine line between whether a company can do something by itself and whether it *should.* Sure, it might make sense to have Joan from accounting design the holiday card to save a few dollars, but having her do the company annual report might be a different story and should be left to the design firm that has always done it.

The other part of sourcing with DIY Gen Z is when they do go to the outside world for information.

Jonah, do you want me to add kale to your smoothie?

For sure. Did you know that kale literally dissolves all unhealthy cells throughout your body?

I know it's healthy for you, but last time I walked through the produce aisle it was labeled as a miracle drug. Who told you this?

Foodbabe.

Who's that?

She's a blogger with ninety-seven thousand followers.

Is she a scientist?

I have no idea.

When my generation researches something, like most folks we go to Google. We then will click on the top two, maybe three, links and get what we need. If not Google, we will put a request out to our personal network and usually within a few minutes get some answers and move on.

The challenge with Gen Z is that access and credibility don't always go hand in hand. In our book *The M-Factor,* we discussed how Millennials' use of social media put an end to the expert as we knew it. Suddenly you wouldn't trust a movie critic to tell you what movie to see; you can ask your network. Why ask a travel expert where to take a trip? You simply ask the same people who told you what movie to see. You used to ask Julia Child or Betty Crocker how to bake something; now you simply tap into the hundreds of people you're connected with on Facebook.

Gen Z only knows a world where everyone and anyone can be an "expert." In fact, a Nielsen study found that 83 percent of Gen Z trusts recommendations from their peers the most. That's opposed to 66 percent trusting consumer opinions posted online and 66 percent trusting editorial content, such as newspaper articles. That's fine if they want to know where to dine or what beach is best for surfing. However, it's another thing if random friends are giving Gen Z input on how to do their job.

ROGER GOODELL
NFL Commissioner

What is the most important quality you will look for in your future boss?

TOP RESPONSE: To be my mentor and be fair

Gen Z's DIY attitude will definitely change the dynamic of the employee-boss relationship. Just ask teachers who have been working with Gen Z for years. It used to be you went to school and your teacher's job was to disseminate information.

Gen Zers don't see it that way, which has forced the role of the teacher to change. Brenda Cassellius is the commissioner of education in our home state of Minnesota. She explained: "Teachers are just now figuring this out and are still constrained by state standards, assessments, and accountability systems. We are stuck in methods of schooling that have outlived their effectiveness. Today it is bigger and deeper than the teacher being the keeper and deliverer of knowledge and a set of skills; they need to understand that students see the knowledge as fluid, too. This makes traditional front-of-the-classroom teaching less effective."

Melissa Kondrick is a middle school math teacher in Pleasanton, California. She has a master's degree in education curriculum and instruction. She has embraced technology in the classroom. She explained: "We have to meet Gen Z where they are if we want to engage with them. You can't just take printed materials and repurpose them online. It needs to be interactive and ideally gamified to keep their attention. Just like adults, students want content that is fun, interesting, or real. This is how they learn best. But even more than the right use of technology and methodology, teachers themselves need to understand their role. This would be my biggest heads-up to bosses when Gen Z hits the workplace. The older model was 'sage on the stage,' where the teacher stood in front of the classroom and 'deposited' knowledge to students. There was only one 'right answer.' Since they were the one with all of the knowledge, they belonged up front. Now, the model is 'guide on the side,' where often the students are collaborating in small groups and/or looking at a screen, not the teacher. Our job is to help coach or guide them through the information. We focus on developing problem-solving skills."

Most teachers have dealt with this evolution, and most have had to learn how to put their egos aside. However, bosses who have worked hard to make it to the top might feel a slight

MARLEE MATLIN
Actress

What do you need from the older generations to be successful at work?

TOP RESPONSE: Be a coach or mentor

bruise on their egos when Gen Z doesn't look to them as all-knowing. Kondrick commented, "As for any advice I have for future bosses, realize that Gen Z is very driven. Enjoy being the guide on the side. Sage on stage will only get in their way. This generation is going places."

Millennials were much more collaborative and therefore were quick to knock on their bosses' doors. Though many complained early on, in the end bosses still felt needed. Gen Z, being more independent, will not go knocking as much. As a result, bosses of Gen Zers may not feel as needed, and worse, they may feel disrespected or that they no longer control the flow of information.

Let's be clear: Gen Z might want to do it ourselves, but we will still need our bosses, just like we need our teachers. In our national survey, 94 percent of Gen Z said they trust their supervisor's input more than Yahoo! Answers. We aren't looking to replace our bosses with a search engine. We might not go to our bosses for all of the information. However, just because we can get our hands on information, that doesn't mean we know what to do with it or even if it is the right information.

Bosses will play a different yet critical role. Gen Z will need a lot of help when it comes to verifying and validating. Again, we can learn a lot from Gen Z's current "bosses"—their teachers. In a national study, the vast majority of teachers say that a top priority in today's classrooms should be teaching students how to "judge the quality of online information."

It's one thing if you take someone's recommendation for

dinner and don't like it. It's another if you put the wrong fact in a client proposal.

The study went on to say that Gen Zers were more concerned with finding information than truly analyzing it. Teachers also warned that surface research teaches students to assume that all tasks can be finished quickly and at the last minute.

Remember, searches for Gen Z have always been quick and easy. However, what about the sources that pop up four or five links down or, gasp . . . on page two? Odds are, there are some golden nuggets in these links that could provide pertinent information. Managers will have to teach Gen Z to take the time to get all the information even if that means daring to go where no Gen Zer has gone before—page two.

Kondrick commented, "Sure, Gen Z has a tendency to click on the first links they see, but they also understand the importance of accuracy. Gen Z has learned at a very young age that plagiarizing or misquoting information is a crime. They are sensitive to it. They may want to get the search done fast, but they aren't looking to cheat."

As much as we will need to spend time teaching Gen Z what is and is not considered a valid source, we shouldn't go so far as trying to control the actual search. As tempting as it will be to list the sources that they are allowed to go to, why limit them?

There will be great benefit in letting them do the sourcing themselves. Odds are that they will introduce you to ones that you would never have found had you DIY.

The Rise of the Freelance Economy

The good news is that the DIY generation will show up at work and be very resourceful. The bad news is that they will be so resourceful, they might not show up at all. According to Millennial Branding, 17 percent of Gen Z, versus 11 percent of Millennials, want to start a business.

Before we dismiss this as Gen Z being young and naïve, there is a slight nuance. When the rest of us think of starting and running a business, we think of the classic entrepreneur who builds an empire and all the resources it takes to pull it off.

When Gen Z thinks of starting and running a business, we often think of being a one-man show even with limited resources. What others have called freelancers, we would call true business owners. Recent research states there are more than 53 million freelancers in the United States. It is quickly becoming one of the largest workforces. It's not that we don't hope our business could turn into an empire; it's that it doesn't have to in order to thrive. In other words, we can DIY. My generation doesn't immediately look to flipping burgers or bagging groceries to make money. We have seen how you can string together a bunch of opportunities to make a buck or two. You can sell stuff on eBay, help your parents rent your home on Airbnb, or when you are old enough, drive for Uber, just to name a few. *Harvard Business Review* found that 70 percent of Gen Z teens are working jobs like these.

As Gen Z gets older, they will be even more inclined to come up with their own business opportunities. As easy as it has been to access what they want online, it is just as easy to market online straight to the consumer. Remember, it's the end of the middleman.

If I wanted to start my own company, within two days I could form an LLC, design a logo, build a website, get an 800 number that forwards to my cell, and have business cards in the mail. If I was really in a hurry, I could probably get it done in a day. And as for what Mom and Dad think of it? Good chance it was their idea! Gallup found that 32 percent of Gen Z said they have a parent or guardian who has started a business. My dad has been self-employed my whole life.

Aside from just their parents' support in starting a business, Gen Z is looking to colleges and universities to teach them how to do it themselves. In fact, Northeastern University found that 63 percent of Gen Z want colleges to offer courses in founding or running a business. Let's face it: It would be hard to find an internship at a company that teaches you how to go off on your own.

A big difference between Gen Xers and their Gen Z children starting their own businesses is that there are a lot more systems and organizations in place today that make it easier to go off on your own. Take something as simple as an office. No longer do you either have to work from your dining room table or rent out a lot of office space with big overhead. You can start right in the middle at a collaborative workspace.

This concept has been around for a while and typically involves what's been called an executive center. These centers were originally targeted to executives who wanted to give the impression that they were bigger than they actually were. What has changed is that now these collaborative spaces are big, hip, and filled with everyone from graphic designers to Web app developers to writers to practically any type of freelancer you can imagine.

It's less about looking big and more about being around others who are in the same boat. It provides amazing networking opportunities and camaraderie. Suddenly you walk into a space with hundreds of people buzzing about, and as much as you are DIY, you can't help but feel like you are part of a bigger movement.

WeWork is an American company that is tapping into this movement. It offers shared workspace, community, and services for entrepreneurs, freelancers, start-ups, and small businesses. They have created these cutting-edge spaces that look anything but stuffy and include everything from gyms to funky kitchens to video game rooms. As their mission states, they want to "create a world where people work to make a life, not just a living." Founded in just 2010, WeWork already has 78 locations in 23 cities around the world and has a valuation of $16 billion at the time of writing this book.

Beyond just where you work, there are even better platforms that help DIYs market their skills. Upwork.com is a resource for those doing it themselves to connect with a marketplace. As they promise users, "Find freelancers to tackle any job, any size, any time. Work with someone perfect for your team." It goes on to offer a menu: Web Developers, Mobile Developers, Designers & Creatives, Writers, Virtual Assistants, Customer Service Agents, Sales & Marketing Experts, Accountants & Consultants . . . and more and more and more. Gen Xers would have loved this help when they were starting their own businesses.

Does it work? Traditional IT firms are experiencing a slowdown in growth, while at the same time the number of people hiring independent consultants for large IT projects on Upwork has increased 22 percent over the last year. It seems that companies are realizing that just because they have a big job to do, they don't have to hire a big company.

The bottom line is that Gen Z has seen doing it yourself become very easy. So easy that according to Northeastern University, 42 percent of Gen Z say they intend to work for themselves. That's a big jump from the only 10.1 percent of Americans the U.S. Bureau of Labor Statistics reported were self-employed as of 2015. However, what makes this even more confusing is that going to work somewhere else or doing it yourself isn't black-and-white. In many cases, we will opt to do both.

The Side Hustle

Dad, did you hear about Sam's business selling reflective gear?

Wait. I thought he just got a job.

He did.

Selling reflective gear?

No. He got a job at the marketing firm he interned for before graduating.

So what's the reflective gear?

It's his own business he is doing on the side. He is killing it! He just landed a contract with a construction company that does work on highways. Making big bucks!

What does his employer think?

I'm not sure. What does it matter?

Say "Do the Hustle" to a Boomer and they remember whistling in a nightclub while launching the world's most famous line dance. While Xers might not remember doing the hustle in a nightclub, odds are they recall that one-week rotation in elementary school where they learned the dance in gym. Fast-forward to Gen Z and the only reference *hustle* has to a dance is the one they are doing between their full-time job and their DIY business "on the side."

As the DIY movement has exploded, so too has the concept of the side hustle. A side hustle is the idea of having your own side business while still being gainfully employed. As we've noted, there are so many resources to help you launch and run your own business, that you can even do it while working somewhere else. The idea of moonlighting will be common practice for DIY Gen Z.

Previous generations couldn't fathom having the time for something on the side. If anyone did, it was assumed it would get in the way of their full-time job. However, they didn't have tools to help them get it done on the side. Gen Z will prove that it can get done and it does.

For Traditionalists and Boomers, talking about any other work than one's main job would have been perceived as disloyal. The goal was to show employers that they had your loyalty and mind space 100 percent. Actually for 80 million competing Boomers, the goal was to show 110 percent. When Gen X showed up, employers had a big adjustment. They had to accept that they were number two on the list and that family and friends were going to come first. Xers were not exactly quiet about the fact that, yes, they would be loyal and give due attention to their jobs, but their personal lives would come first. It's not that Boomers didn't care about their family and friends. The landscape was so competitive that if they wanted to keep their job or get ahead, they had to show that they were willing to put work before anything else.

Inc. reports that 75 percent of Gen Z wish their current hobby could become their full-time job. With the arrival of Gen Z, the workplace will have to adjust yet again. So much for losing employees to your competitor; the bigger fear will be losing us to the world of DIY.

Now employers won't just be competing for loyalty and mind space with family and friends, but with side hustles as well. This will not be easy to navigate. Who owns your mind space? It would be hard for an employer to say that they do from 9 a.m. to 5 p.m., since they also know that emails and workloads go way beyond those boundaries. At the same time, employers should receive some degree of loyalty for providing a steady income and benefits.

We're not saying that Traditionalists, Boomers, Xers, or Millennials haven't had side hustles. However, these issues

---

RICHARD DAVIS
CEO of U.S. Bank

If you create your own product/service that results in a success while you work at a company, who should own that intellectual property?

Only 12 percent said the company should own it.
43 percent said it should be co-owned.
40 percent said my invention, my property.

---

haven't surfaced much until now since for previous generations, it was still something you kept on the down-low.

Virgin Hotels realized that a lot of their Gen Z employees had side hustles. While they were working the front desk, housekeeping, waiting tables, etc. for the hotel, they were also models and musicians on the side. Clio Knowles, the vice president of people, said, "We didn't want employees to feel as though they had to hide these side hustles from us. If a modeling opportunity comes up last minute, rather than call in sick, we want the culture to be open and honest and ideally supportive. During the recruiting process we introduced a personal brand exercise that simply asks if they do have other work projects. It's amazing how much the Gen Zers appreciate being asked and love to talk about it. It's just easier if it is all on the table."

As more and more Gen Zers enter the workplace, side hustles

won't be something we try to hide at all. Since the Internet will be how we market our side hustles, we know that finding out about them is only a Google search away. We won't see employers as being threatened at all. In fact, we will likely put our side hustles big and bold on our resume to showcase our entrepreneurial skills that we assume employers will be looking for.

To Compete or Not Compete

Before we say anything else, let us first comment that of course if any employee's side hustle is interfering with getting their job done, then there is nothing to embrace other than an ultimatum. However, there will be a fine line between those side hustles that do and don't compete on a larger scale.

Employers will have to accept that when it comes to ultimate loyalty or mind space, they will be competing and likely not be in first place. The days of Traditionalists and Boomers proving their job is the most important part of their life are over. That's not to say that businesses are doomed. They can and will still get amazing results from their Gen Z employees. In fact, the best approach will be to focus on results. If employees are hitting them, then it shouldn't matter.

At the same time, employers will have to focus on the side hustles themselves. That does matter. Employers will need to know if the side hustle has potential conflict with the business.

This may seem like an obvious conversation, but for my generation, who has seen everyone have them, it might not be as clear. Starting right in the recruiting process, it will be important to ask us if we have a side hustle and what it is. Again, this will not be something we hide behind.

To Compete

Once the side hustle is on the table, the goal will be to assess if it is a threat to the business. For years, companies dealt with this by relying on the infamous noncompete agreement employees signed. The problem over the years was that many of them were hard to enforce in a court of law and much of the important detail was left in the fine print. In the end a lot of time and money has been wasted. Savvy companies are doing more than having employees just sign a noncompete in the onboarding process; they are talking about what exactly is in the fine print and what it means.

Industries such as high tech have been dealing with this for even longer than Gen Z has been alive. It is beyond the norm for software engineers to have something going on the side. Leading-edge, successful companies like Google and Facebook not only know this, but also encourage it. The feeling is that if engineers are exploring new interests, they are expanding their minds and keeping things fresh—not just for the engineers themselves, but for the companies, too. Google is famous for its policy of workers spending 20 percent of their time on interests outside the job. That being said, it works until what they are exploring can actually be monetized or compete with the company. The company then makes it clear as day that the exploration belongs to it. In many situations, it becomes a win-win. A perfect example is MRY (formerly Mr. Youth), a New York–based technology and creative agency. Like Google and Facebook, they push their employees to pursue their individual passions and talents. For example, Brandon Evans went to CEO and founder Matt Britton with an idea to create an advertising tech platform that allows brands the ability to harness the power of influencers. Rather than tell Brandon to go back to his day job, Matt encouraged Brandon to go for it, and even invested in the idea. Today this idea, known as Crowdtap, has been spun off into its own company, with fifty-plus employees and millions in annual revenues. Best of all, Brandon was promoted to CEO to run the venture. As Matt explained, "In this day and age, employees are going to become their own enterprise. The smartest thing to do is embrace it. By allowing them to invest time and energy into their own creative passions, you get a driven and dedicated employee in return. Think of it as the modern-day job contract."

While bigger companies can afford to litigate or take the risk if necessary, it is trickier for many of the tech start-ups. These companies are usually in a race to be first to market. They expect the days of Traditionalists and Boomers, where your job is your life. Whether or not they can afford litigation, they definitely cannot afford any distraction.

According to Dan Grosh, managing partner at Calibre One, a global executive search firm for public and emerging growth tech companies, "Side hustles have definitely had an impact on executive recruitment. I have seen some deals fall through where a candidate leaving a big company to work at a start-up comes to the table with a side hustle and the deal falls flat. These are candidates that any start-up would dream to have as an employee. However, the start-up wants that employee to be all in one hundred percent. The problem is that it has gotten really hard to define one hundred percent. With so many high-tech tools and solutions at employees' fingertips, it has become even harder to find candidates who don't have side hustles."

It's one thing to be talking about a DIY side hustle that impacts the business. What about when it doesn't?

To Not Compete

Jonah, I just got a call from our client who told me they are buying T-shirts from us for the speech.

Isn't that cool?

What are you talking about?

Well, she told me that they were looking for a great giveaway gift for attendees and I suggested T-shirts.

Okay, it's one thing to suggest them. It's another to sell them.

Dad, it is so easy to order shirts from a screen printer and mark them up.

I didn't realize we were now in the T-shirt business.

Who said anything about "we"?

If you are General Mills and an employee makes cereal on the side that's a problem. However, if he/she is making pottery on the side, it's probably not going to be a big threat. In these situations, maybe there's an update to the old phrase, "If you can't beat them, promote them."

We all know that mom or dad who walks around the office taking orders for their kid's Girl Scout cookies. Granted, who doesn't love a good Thin Mint, right? And what kid doesn't love when their parent taps into a built-in marketplace and comes home that night with a page full of orders?!

Well, what employee engaged in a side hustle wouldn't love the ability to tap into that very same marketplace?

If William from accounting has a side business making cool mailboxes, why not help him sell them around the company so he loves his day job all the more? Odds are there are more than just mailboxes that could be up for sale. Jan crochets, Erik paints, Stu does flower arrangements, Sharon sews curtains, and so on. We know they are out there.

Gen Z will love to see a company not just embrace our DIY side hustles, but promote them. It might be the best recruitment and retention tool companies have.

DIY Zingers!

- Define how handoffs and check-ins will work with this independent generation.
- Be open to new sources of information and expertise.
- Coach Gen Z on how to establish the credibility and capacity of sources they identify.
- Keep bosses in the loop, even if they aren't the main source of direction or expertise.
- Watch for Gen Z to be entrepreneurial and put that to work internally rather than lose them.
- Be prepared to manage "side hustle" issues as they arrive. Coach managers on the parameters they need to know.

DRIVEN

You ready, buddy?

I think so.

What do you mean you think so? It's your first baseball game. You've got this!

I just hope I hit the ball.

Like we've been practicing, just keep your eye on it. You've been connecting so well. Just remember, if you strike out, it happens. Brush it off and get back up to the plate next time. You can't—

I know, don't let it get in my head. You've told me.

Look, the only way to win is to score runs.

Yup. I know.

We're almost there. How about I put on the perfect song?

■ ■ ■

I still remember this car ride down to the baseball field for my first game. I was seven years old. My dad was so serious and proceeded to play "Eye of the Tiger" while pumping his fist. When we got to the field he made me punch the air to the beat of the song. You bet he wanted to be sure I was ready to kick some baseball butt!

Oh how I wish Jonah was exaggerating, but I own it. But here's what happened. We got to the field and it ends up I'm the only Gen X dad and the others are all Boomers. I didn't get the memo that the speech I gave—okay, drilled into Jonah—was a no-no.

The way Boomers saw this was definitely different than how Gen Xers did. Jonah was greeted by Coach Rob, who bent down with his hands on his knees and said, "Hey, little buddy. I'm Coach Rob. Welcome to the Sidewinders. How are you doing?"

Jonah responded, "Well, I'm good. I just hope I can hit the ball."

I gave him the old dad nod of the head with a serious look and squinting eyes. You know, Mr. Tough Guy. Only to see Coach Rob reply, "Aw, buddy, there's nothing to be nervous about. In fact, when you get to the plate, you get to swing and swing and swing until you hit the ball. We don't do three strikes. So there's nothing to be nervous about!"

I looked at Coach Rob waiting for the punch to my shoulder telling me he was just kidding, but he just smiled and kept right on going. "The way it will work is that everyone on the team will get their turn at bat and then we take the outfield. We don't—"

"Wait," I interrupted. "Everyone gets a turn at bat each inning?"

"You bet! Isn't that great?" he answered.

"What about three outs?"

"We don't have three outs. This way, everyone gets a chance at bat." Now I knew he wasn't kidding. I fell silent.

"And finally, little buddy," he told Jonah, "team rules: We don't keep score. Let's just have some fun. Okay? I'll let you get your things together, then come meet the teammates in the dugout."

As Coach Rob headed to the field, I looked around to see if any dads were protesting, but they all seemed happy sitting in their lawn chairs reading the paper, drinking coffee, and waiting for the "game" to begin.

The whole time I was trying to listen to the coach, I could see my dad out of the corner of my eye: his jaw was in his lap. I was just so relieved he didn't say anything. As soon as the coach walked away, my dad mumbled, "Okay . . . it looks like we'll be here until January. Do your best." He then leaned down and whispered, "Jonah, don't worry. I'll keep score."

This is one of my favorite memories since it was one of those moments when I realized that things were changing. For Coach Rob and many of the Boomer dads on the team, it was all about building self-esteem with their Millennial kids and making sure that everyone is a winner. But for me, it was a wake-up call that I would be parenting and raising Jonah very differently.

I saw no problem with the kids striking out. I wanted to beat the other team, and for sure didn't think they all deserved trophies. As mentioned in the "Mom & Dad" chapter, Gen X parents have always tried to hammer into their Gen Z kids that there are winners and losers.

On top of this parental influence, Gen Z experienced a severe recession in which they saw many around them fight hard to keep what they had worked so hard to earn. In addition, they have seen many Millennials not only stalled in their careers, but also saddled with a lot of debt. Throw in a rate of change that is hard to keep up with and Gen Z feels immense pressure as well as impatience to move rapidly ahead.

It is no wonder that Gen Z is a very driven generation.

It's important to deconstruct this driven trait so that we not only understand it, but even more important, know how to manage it.

Motivated to Win

A big difference between Millennials and Gen Z is that Gen Zers are more competitive. In our national survey, 72 percent of Gen Z said they are competitive with people doing the same job. Millennials were told by Boomer parents that if everyone works together, everyone can benefit and there doesn't have to be just one winner. The result was an extremely collaborative generation that teamed up to get the job done. As Millennials step into management, they will have to learn how to harness Gen Z's competitive drive rather than see it as not being

MARILYN NELSON
Former Chair and CEO of Carlson, Radisson Hotels

Do you believe business can be a powerful force for good?

Yes: 93 percent
No: 7 percent

For those who feel business can be a powerful force for good, why?

TOP RESPONSE: Businesses have the ability to make positive change and improve society.

For those who feel business cannot be a powerful force for good, why not?

TOP RESPONSE: Greed and corruption

a team player. Ideally they can put it to work to go the extra mile.

If any generation is going to appreciate a good competitive spirit, it's the generation that was defined by competing to stand out—the Boomers. Boomers will understand Gen Z's driven trait and how to use competitiveness as a true motivator.

Boomers have always been the most competitive generation. At all times Boomers knew not just where they stood on the corporate ladder, but where everyone around them stood. It was a race to the top of the ladder and the higher you would climb, the fewer rungs there were to land on. It was always a fierce competition!

When it came time to raise children of their own, Boomers decided that constant competing wasn't the best way to get ahead. Instead they focused on telling their Millennial children to put their best effort forward regardless of the outcome. As long as you try your best, you'll be just fine.

The new goal was to bring your own special assets to the table, team up with everyone, and not worry as much about competing with them. Millennials were so used to all projects in college being done in a group and even getting group grades. This is how we ended up with Boomer coaches like Rob, who wasn't focused on three strikes or outs, but rather on everyone working together.

Thus the invention of the famous participation award, which was more about celebrating the effort put in than the final result. This may or may not have worked on the baseball field, but it has been difficult for the Coach Robs of the world in the office.

The reality is that at work you don't get more than three strikes, not everyone gets a turn at bat, we care a lot about the competition, and we definitely keep score. Boomers and Xers have struggled to create a sense of urgency with the Millennials, who weren't as motivated to win. Many are so quick to roll their eyes at Millennials for getting ninth-place trophies. Let's remember, they weren't the ones giving them out and don't know a different world.

Now, with competitive Gen Z showing up, collaborative Millennials will have to think twice. Giving a Gen Zer a "participation award" will definitely fall flat. After all, our parents were the first ones to throw

DAVID FOSTER

16-Time Grammy Award–Winning Music Producer

Are you optimistic about the future of the world?

Yes: 70 percent
No: 30 percent

For those who are not optimistic about the future of the world, why?

TOP 3 RESPONSES

Too many problems that aren't being solved
Destruction of the environment
The world is full of hate and greed

them away. Our Gen X parents have taught us the art of winning. How to break down your goals and what it takes to reach for them.

At the same time, they have also taught us the art of losing. The message has always been that if you learn something from the experience, it ultimately is a win. That said, we may have learned how to lose at baseball, but losing on the job will be new for us. Gen Z will want managers to take the time to talk to us about what we have learned from it so that it not only doesn't happen again, but in fact drives us to do even better next time.

With Speed Come Demons

The younger generation moving at a more rapid pace is not a new thing. It's a tale that's been told. Whatever generation is the youngest, they are typically accused of everything from talking too fast to walking too fast to just being extremely impatient. With Gen Z, thanks to the rate of change and advancements of technology, every trait in this book has some relation to Gen Z's need for speed.

Whether it's FOMO and the push to get updated information as often as possible or growing up in a phigital world where download speeds have eliminated the line between physical and digital, speed plays a role. Consider "Realistic," with Gen Z seeing how fast the world is moving and needing to stay ahead of the curve, or "DIY" and how doing it yourself rather than waiting for someone else is often fastest and easiest.

And now with "Driven," Gen Z will speed ahead at a pace that will be challenging to manage.

For starters, Gen Z is wired to make decisions at lightning speeds. Their drive to get ahead will keep them from overthinking things. They will do what they can to keep the momentum going. As we learned in "FOMO," when you are less fearful of making a mistake, you simply know that if the decision wasn't the right one, you pivot, make a new one, and continue to cruise ahead. When everyone is under the gun, this can be a good thing.

However, there will be plenty of times when it is not a great idea to make a decision too fast. This is something that managers will have to pay attention to. Gen Z's main objective is to make a decision and drive ahead. That's how they've been conditioned. It will be harder for them to imagine leaving work or logging off and just sleeping on it for a night, letting all of the information actually marinate.

They might miss out on what could be the most valuable asset of all: their own opinion. It's one thing to come up with an answer; it's another to develop an opinion or suggestion. We need to be sure to encourage and create cultures for Gen Z to take the time to form their own opinions, think them through, bounce them off people, and not feel like they have to make decisions too quickly.

For years smart organizations have been creating time to explore, think, and even daydream. For more than a decade Google has allotted 20 percent of time and 3M 10 percent for thinking and creating . . . even if that means staring at the wall for a while. They know that some of the best ideas can actually come from "down" time. They also know that it just sets the right tone for their culture. The mentality to "work outside the box" is ingrained in cultures that have these initiatives. As 3M put it, "Creativity needs freedom."

Innovation really has two aspects. One is thinking, ruminating, and researching so disparate pieces come together. Then there's the idea where you don't overanalyze and just get something out to the marketplace. The goal with Gen Z is to help find the balance.

As cool as this "down" time sounds, it will not feel natural to my generation. In fact, for driven Gen Zers, just sitting around "thinking" could actually feel wasteful. We will need help in seeing that this downtime is actually useful when it comes to true innovation.

Another speed demon with Gen Z's drive to get ahead is that many traditional careers will seem too slow and archaic to pursue. Careers or opportunities that the other generations saw as providing safety and security, Gen Z might feel different about. Take a job in marketing, for example. Where competitive Boomers fought hard to work on iconic, long-standing brands, Gen Z will likely see those as stagnant, boring, and even risky.

A Boomer would feel like they won the lottery if they landed on the Cheerios brand, whereas Gen Z's drive would have them more interested in a new organic brand without sugar and loaded with protein and fiber. Pressure will be on for companies to figure out new value propositions for lines of business that have always been their bread and butter. For Gen Z, however, these lines of business might feel too slow.

Regardless of what brand or line of business Gen Z works on, the biggest speed demon of all will be their career paths. We all know that the days of staying in one position for months or years without advancement began a slow death with Gen X and was eventually laid to rest with Millennials. Traditionalists came of age when there were strict structures and guidelines for how employees advanced in their careers.

There was only one direction and that was up. For example, it was crystal clear that you started as an associate for five years, then would move to manager for three years, then director for five years and so on. Boomers came along and had no choice but to accept that careers moved at this pace. If they didn't like it, there were enough others to go around who would stay the course. The only way they could shorten the timeline was if there was a merger, expansion, or acquisition; then they could try to seize the opportunity to break out and up.

Then came Gen Xers, who saw the end of lifetime employment at one place as well as the end of the job contract. They basically saw the end of long-term security. There wasn't the same incentive to pay dues. Those companies that didn't revisit dues-paying cultures found that Xers moved up the ladder anyway—only somewhere else. With Millennials, dues paying became even more foreign amid the push to pay more attention to skill sets than tenure when deciding whom to promote. In our book *The M-Factor*, we reported that 82 percent of Millennials who said they were unhappy at their jobs believed that career paths ascended too gradually where they worked.

Now we will have driven Gen Zers, who also will want to move, move, move! On one hand, we will all want to retain Gen Zers after investing in training them and will not want to see them go. On the other hand, if they are constantly becoming competent at something only as a way to move on, it wastes resources as well as human capacity for the organization. Organizations will need to keep them learning and growing to keep them at all.

As driven as Gen Z will be, it is time we put on the brakes when we feel it is necessary. With so many leaders fearing that Millennials would leave, the last thing they were willing to do was tell a Millennial to slow down. Yes, Gen Z will expect the world of work to fly at lightning speed. However, there is nothing wrong with telling them that sometimes things will just take time. The key is to explain, or even better, mentor them on why. Remember, they are used to getting straightforward information without a lot of sugarcoating.

For Gen Z, as soon as we have mastered a task, we assume we are ready to move on. It's a lot like the video games we grew up playing, where as soon as you were good enough at a skill, you moved up to the next level, which was harder. You never stay on the same level and just play; you keep on moving. It will be confusing to us to stay on the same level once we are good at something.

My generation can learn a lot when it comes to expectations about how fast careers move in the office. The key will be to explain that even if we aren't "moving" we are still driving forward. The way to do this is to focus on pointing out how what we are learning along the way is helping us prepare for our future and will always pay off. That way, we won't feel stalled at all.

However, as much as our fast-paced driven attitude will be challenging when it comes to our career paths, perhaps it can be a good thing when taking products or services to market. We know the pressure is on to beat the competition to the marketplace and we are wired, or driven, to get there first. We have been conditioned to always be looking for a faster route.

Gen Z can be a go-to resource at work for ideas on how to pick up the pace. We will be a set of fresh eyes. If we can order something on Amazon and have it at our door within twenty-four hours, only imagine the reaction Gen Z will have when we're told that prototyping alone will take six months. Maybe it won't have to.

Training for the Journey

When you're a generation with a competitive spirit who wants to move at a fast pace, you need to be in the best shape possible. Everyone has heard of the saying "It's a marathon, not a sprint."

My generation looks at our careers as a marathon that *is* a sprint. We know we will have to keep pushing forward as best and as fast as we can. We also know that we will be at it for a long time. We don't anticipate stopping to work. What this means is that my generation is very aware of staying healthy.

Sure, when you're young you feel invincible, but we have also been taught that it doesn't mean our bodies are unbreakable. In her book *The Sleep Revolution*, Arianna Huffington explains that at my age, I should be getting 8–10 hours of sleep. That's not happening! I have to be up at 6 a.m., which would put me in bed between 8 and 10 p.m. I can't think of one friend who is lights-out by 10 p.m. This is one area where Gen Z has some work, or should I say sleep, to do. However, we are not failing completely.

Growing up, we witnessed the wake-up call that fat is not the demon, sugar is. We know that the Centers for Disease Control and Prevention predicts that 1 in 3 Americans will have diabetes by 2050, when we will be in the prime of our careers. Gen X and Millennial breakfast heroes such as Cap'n Crunch and Trix the Rabbit have become pseudo drug dealers for Gen Z, pushing sugar as though it were cocaine. In a Nielsen survey 41 percent of my generation said we would be willing to pay a premium for "healthier" products. That compares with 32 percent of Millennials.

JIMMY JOHN LIAUTAUD
Founder and CEO of Jimmy John's

Are you willing to work longer hours and harder than your fellow Gen Z rock stars to reach your goals?

Yes: 88 percent
No: 7 percent

We have seen the negative results of not taking care of ourselves and a lot of grown-ups have been trying to get us to make healthier choices. As our Gen X parents inevitably experience that first health scare or challenge, our efforts will only intensify. From First Lady Michelle Obama to Jamie Oliver the message is loud and clear to live a healthier life, or else. We see activities like sports as a tool for health instead of just playing games.

While the teenage years are typically seen as the time for experimentation and reckless behavior, this is proving to be less the case with Gen Z. Awareness campaigns have worked and drug use, alcohol consumption, and smoking are at their lowest levels in decades.

Robin Koval, CEO and president of Truth Initiative and co-author of *Grit to Great*, has been leading the charge when it comes to Gen Z living a healthy life. Truth Initiative, formerly known as the American Legacy Foundation, has been working to inspire tobacco-free lives. It began with Xers in the first decade of the century. "Our ability to tap into a generation's personality has been continually successful for Truth over the years. For Gen X," explained Koval, "it was all about rebellion and anti-institution. Our messages focused on how the tobacco companies were roping Xers in and that they needed to fight back by not smoking. For Gen Zers, we are now talking to them about being the generation to end smoking for good." The name of the campaign is "Finish It!"

Koval said, "We know that Gen Z is worried about the health of themselves and our world at large. We are not surprised that we are seeing risky behaviors decline with this generation. However, we still have work to do. We have had to figure out the best way to tap into their generational personality, no different than how we had to do with their Gen X parents. While we uncovered many tactics, the biggest one that connected with this generation was that Gen Z is more about what they can be for, rather than against. The anti-institution message that worked with Gen X didn't resonate with Gen Z. They resonated with becoming the generation to end smoking. A victory is more appealing to them."

As we now watch Gen Z head into the workforce, first and foremost, leaders will need to know how important health and wellness are to Gen Z. It will need to be more than just offering the best health-care benefits or a workout room. Gen Z is extremely holistic about their lives and will be looking at a lot more.

Gen Zers know they need to stay conditioned if they are going to compete to be successful and get ahead. When asked in our national survey what the most important employee

JAMIE OLIVER FOOD FOUNDATION

Would you be willing to start a food revolution in your workplace?

Yes: 61 percent
No: 39 percent

benefit was, Gen Z said health-care coverage, even over time off! They have heard the horror stories of the older generations not having medical coverage and do not want to roll the dice. Many benefits related to health and well-being that were mostly just considered nice to have by previous generations will be the best investment companies can make to attract and retain Gen Z. Best of all, many of them don't cost much for employers, considering the retention benefits they yield.

Health is on Gen Z's radar and will need to be on employers' as well if they want to connect with us. Whether it is membership to a local health club or setting up your own exercise room, we will notice. Even the food choices for the cafeteria, the snacks served at meetings, and the quality of the air in the building are on our radar. So is whether we are getting enough sleep. In fact, in Huffington's sleep book, she talks about colleges and universities having designated nap rooms. Maybe it's not a bad idea for corporate America. Living a healthy life has been a big part of conversations at home and at school. It will only feel natural to keep talking about it at work.

The bottom line is that for driven Gen Z, leaders had better offer health and wellness not as a benefit, but as part of the daily regimen.

Independent Operators

I'm so annoyed. I have to go to Will's house to finish our business economics project.

Why are you annoyed?

Luke is always late, Morgan doesn't get it, and Zach doesn't even care.

Can't you talk to them?

It doesn't make a difference. Just such a waste of my time and this project is 20 percent of our grade. It would be so much easier if I could do it all myself.

One of the ways this driven generation has learned to get to a finish line fast and efficiently has been to do it themselves. As we discussed in "DIY," 71 percent of Gen Z believes that the saying "If you want it done right, then do it yourself" definitely applies to them.

Gen Z's push for independence should not be a shocker since much of their "training" has come from their Gen X parents. Xers had grown up with two working parents, of which many were divorced. Xers were the latchkey kids who came home to an empty house and truly fended for themselves.

They took this independence with them right on into the workplace and found that some of their biggest clashes with

MARK PARKER
President and CEO of Nike

What can Generation Z learn from the best sports teams?

TOP 3 RESPONSES
Teamwork
Perseverance
Sportsmanship

Boomers involved their desire to work at their own pace and in their own space. There were so many policies and procedures that Boomers had set up for how work gets done that Xers tried to figure out how to avoid some of the bureaucracy. Xers wanted to fly under the radar. Boomers who were finally in leadership positions and wanted control were not comfortable with it.

At first Xers got a bad rap for not being team players, but eventually Boomers and Xers figured it out. As long as Boomers could spend the time in the handoff being very clear what was being assigned, what the roles were, when the project was due, in what format, and at what points to check in, it was okay for the Xer to go away and do their thing. In fact, over time Boomers came to appreciate it and even enjoy it. They got something off their desk and didn't have to think about it until the next check-in. It took a while for Boomers to understand that it wasn't about rejecting them, but that Xers worked best independently and not being micromanaged.

So as we said, we shouldn't be surprised that when Xers raised their kids, it felt natural to instill a sense of independence.

Sure, a big part of this comes back to how our parents raised us, but it also feels like the most strategic way to operate. With our competitive nature, we are more driven to just want to work by ourselves. Group projects feel risky rather than helpful since someone else can have such a dramatic impact on your final result. This is a big concern to my generation and me. Just as our Gen X parents' independence caused gaps at work, so too might ours. Everything we hear about Millennials has to do with how collaborative they are. We see operating solo as the strategic move and Millennials see operating in groups that way. Neither is right or wrong, but they are on opposite ends of the spectrum. Millennials will be our frontline managers and could see our push for independence as being disrespectful.

Jonah is right. Millennials love to collaborate and will not like Gen Z's independent nature. Again, we shouldn't be surprised. Boomers raised their Millennial kids to be team players. They involved their kids in major household decisions, from where to go on vacation to what house to buy. They truly collaborated with their kids and checked in on everything.

They hadn't, however, really thought about what would happen when this collaborative crew showed up at work. In actuality, Boomers had gotten used to Xers getting a handoff and practically disappearing until the next check-in. Suddenly

Millennials showed up and were knocking on their boss's door every five minutes. Imagine the irony that so many Boomers complained about Millennials' need for constant handholding and check-ins, yet that was exactly how they had raised Millennials.

History might just repeat itself when independent Gen Zers show up. Now that Xers are in leadership positions with a lot more responsibility, they will likely be taken back by Gen Zers who want to fly under the radar. Imagine the irony when Xers complain about Gen Z going rogue when in fact that is exactly how Xers raised them.

With the likelihood of history repeating itself, hopefully we can learn from it. Millennials will have to realize first and foremost that Gen Z is not rejecting them or their teams. At the same time, with Millennials now in management, they can spend time teaching Gen Z how to collaborate at work. The workforce has come to rely on Millennials' ability to collaborate. However, just because that worked for Millennials does not mean it will work best for Gen Z.

Just as Boomers came to appreciate how Xers would go away and get the job done, hopefully Millennials will learn to feel this way about Gen Z. That said, as mentioned in "DIY," we have to be careful that Gen Z doesn't go too rogue. Gen Z will be way more willing to take risks than Xers were. You don't want them to go away only for you to check in way later and find out your one assignment has turned into a new company initiative that looks nothing like your handoff.

Protectors of Privacy

As a driven generation, Gen Z has grown up to believe that if you keep things more private, there is less of a chance of things getting in your way, or even worse, getting you in trouble. My dad has always said to me, "Even a fish can't get caught if it keeps its mouth shut." Part of this comes from growing up in a world where it's a lot harder to keep and even protect personal information.

When people hear that Gen Z is a private generation, they are at first confused because all they see is our heads buried in our phones all day, communicating with people. How could we be private? Yes, we are constantly communicating, but we are very calculating about whom we are communicating with.

A perfect example is Facebook. This was the platform that so many Millennials embraced and launched. They share information about their lives with everyone and now it is so common to log on at any time and hear about the size of someone's fish they caught at the cabin or how wonderful their shrimp fried rice tasted at dinner.

Our Gen X parents watched many Millennials share too much and even have it haunt them when they showed up at the office. It was drilled into our heads to be very careful what we post and who sees it. In fact, according to JWT Intelligence, 82 percent of Gen Zers think carefully about what they put on social media. Since 2012, reports have shown that teens' use of Facebook has steadily dropped.

Gen Z likes to create anonymous and more private content

ED NORTON
Activist and Actor

If you were envisioning your perfect working balance, what percentage of your working time would you want to be left alone to work on your own and what percentage of time would you want to be working collaboratively with others, in a group effort?

Left alone to work on my own: 55 percent of the time

Work collaboratively with others in a group effort: 45 percent of the time

through apps like Snapchat, Whisper, Yik Yak, or Secret. We still post what we are up to, but we are very selective about who sees it as well as how long it is posted. When asked to rank the security of various social media platforms, Gen Z ranked Snapchat the most secure and Facebook the least.

On one hand, Gen Z's push for privacy will catch the others off guard because they see the generation as being so social. But on the other hand, it will be welcomed. Boomers and Xers often found themselves cringing at the Monday morning meeting as Millennials shared all the dirty details about what happened over the weekend.

Our national study found that 70 percent of Gen Z would rather share personal information with their pet than with their boss. You can bet that Gen Z will not be sharing all the dirty details from the weekend, and good luck finding any of it online. Again, it was hammered into us at all times that people are watching what we say or post.

Beyond just the Monday morning meeting, Gen Z's more private nature could be a good thing. Leaders struggled with Millennials when they had to spend a lot more time than they had anticipated explaining to them about organizational privacy. There were too many stories of Millennials innocently sharing happenings at work with their network, only for the post to give a leg up to a competitor who got wind of it. That said, as much as Gen Z is more private, we can't assume they will know how this plays out at work. Just as parents have had to be clear about what the rules and expectations are, so too should bosses. The good news is that Gen Z's instinct is already to hold back.

This could all be well and good if Gen Z doesn't share information with the outside world, but it could become problematic if lack of sharing plays out within the organization. Sure, it's one thing if Gen Z doesn't share everything that went down over the weekend, but it's another if they aren't sharing critical information about how work gets done.

Gen Z is so driven to get ahead that companies will have to keep an eye on knowledge hoarding. We saw this with Boomers as they neared retirement. With the threat of younger, lower-cost employees coming in, many Boomers knew that knowledge would be power and therefore they did not share it. Years of crucial knowledge went with them when they walked out the door and many companies did not have time or money to get it back. Or, in drastic situations, a Boomer had to suddenly leave a job and there was no one who could jump in because so much of the knowledge had not been shared.

Gen Z's instinct to be private will have them believing that they should keep things close to the vest rather than share it. Given that they will be more competitive than previous generations, they too will feel pressure to be relevant. We will have to monitor Gen Z keeping pertinent information too private and be clear about our expectations around what they are to share about their work, with whom, and why.

The other aspect to monitoring privacy is to be sure that Gen Z's driven attitude doesn't lead them to bury mistakes. Yes, it's true that they don't fear failing. However, that doesn't mean they will be eager to share when they actually do fail. They would rather put it behind them and move on like after a bad test score.

Gen Z has not been primed to share bad results. Think about how we post on social media. We only post the best picture, which has often been retouched with the ultimate headline in hopes of only getting thumbs-up. If the picture doesn't get the reactions we had hoped for, you'd better bet the photo is taken down.

Private. Keep Out.

Probably the biggest jolt that Gen Z's private nature will cause is to how our offices are set up. Gen Zers take their need for privacy from the digital realm to the physical.

With the arrival of collaborative Millennials came the redesign of many offices. Walls have come down, cubicles have turned into tables, and many have embraced the open office concept. Boomers who spent their whole career fighting for an office with a real door and ultimately the one in the corner have had to move to flexible spaces where offices with a door are for anyone who occasionally needs a little privacy. Xers who liked any door since it meant they could work in their own space have really had to adjust. As for Millennials, they love it. It's like working in a dorm.

Gen Z? Not so much. In our national survey, 69 percent of Gen Z would rather have their own workspace than share it with someone else. Only 8 percent wanted to share a workspace or have an open office concept. This isn't about wanting our own office space as a status symbol; it's about our drive to get ahead and keep our nose to the grindstone and other noses out of our business. In fact, 35 percent of Gen Z would rather share socks than an office space.

We recently were on a tour of an office after a speech and this Millennial said, "How cool is this, we don't have offices. Just these large working hubs where you sit down wherever you feel like working that day." It looked like an airport to me. The most embarrassing part, however, was when my dad actually asked if they had stall doors in their bathrooms.

Keith Alper, CEO and founder of Nitrous Effect, which specializes in marketing, digital, entertainment, events, and employee engagement, commented, "In our business, we have

BLAKE MYCOSKIE
Founder of TOMS Shoes

What would you change about work today?

TOP RESPONSE: More flexibility around where and when I work

been hiring a lot of Gen Zers. One of the biggest differences we see with our Gen Z employees is that they are fine with the occasional team meeting, but when it comes time to rolling up their sleeves, they want their own private space. Many ask if they can work remotely. At first we thought that they didn't like us, but we just had to adapt to the fact that they want to work in new ways."

It's not that companies will have to build up walls again and feel that they have wasted everything they invested in the open office concept. In fact, it will be great training for Gen Z to learn how to work more collaboratively and in teams. However, there will have to be some adjustments. Gen Z might ask for more private workspaces for when they do get to go away and just get it done. Part of it might be letting them go even farther than the four walls, to the local coffee shop or even their own apartment. And remember, it's not that they don't like others, it's that they prefer to work by themselves.

Driver's Ed

As driven as Gen Z is, they are definitely open to being mentored. Just as Boomers have done a stellar job with their Millennial children, so too have Gen Xers with Gen Z when it comes to opening up lines of communication. So much of Gen Z's formative years were spent watching everyone around them deal with a bad economy, financial uncertainty, or a rocky job market. Luckily they had Gen X parents who showed them how to cope, often by helping them gain access to just the right resource.

Gen Z is used to being mentored. From parents to teachers to aunts, uncles, coaches, college consultants, rabbis, priests, counselors, neighbors, and more . . . Gen Z has been blessed with adults who are interested in their well-being. We know that Millennials' coaching sessions consisted of a lot of self-esteem building. Sure, Gen Z had their pats on the back, but there was also no holding back. At a young age, they learned to be very resilient. After all, they've had to.

It's not that we thrive in those tough times or even enjoy them; it's that we have learned to survive in them. In many ways, we aren't scared of them, either. We like to take risks, but we also want to be as prepared as possible. What has always helped is that our parents have not held back or protected us from what is going on. In fact, they have learned that the best thing is to expose us to as much as possible so we can feel confident that we know what to do.

There is no doubt that this resiliency will serve Gen Z well. However, they are still new to the workplace and we can't forget that. Yes, they can cope, but that doesn't equate to knowing just what to do when the going gets tough. As managers, we don't have to wait until tough times happen; we can share with them when things weren't going well and what the company did. About the time the company opened up an office in a new country and what that entailed. The more we can expose them to different scenarios, the better they will be at driving ahead.

If there is one thing that will require the most driver's ed for this generation, it's a dose of patience. It's no surprise that the youngest ones on the block are being told to chill out, but with Gen Z the message about being patient will be more important than ever before. Millennials were excited to get ahead and had endless energy. Their focus on collaborating rather than competing allowed them to live in the moment, more than Gen Z would be able or willing to. What others would see as just a bad third quarter, Gen Z might see as a death sentence.

As we've discussed, our driven personalities have made us more competitive, fiercely independent, and risk taking, as well as conditioned to make fast decisions. Telling Gen Z to just relax or be patient is going to be tough. We might not be as good at understanding that some things just take time. It will have to be explained to Gen Z that some "wins" can take months and months, if not years. Rather than write us off as being immature, manage our expectations. You may also have to focus on some smaller wins we can have along the way.

Jonah, guess who Mom and I bumped into at the movie last night.

Who?

Coach Rob. Remember him from baseball?

Of course I do.

He was a great coach.

Really? Even though we only won two games that year?

I think I was the only one who actually tracked that.

Oh. That's for sure! Dad, you used to make so much fun of him.

I know. But I do have to say that every time you got in the car you did have a huge smile on your face. You never cared if you won or lost. In fact, you made friends on the other team.

I never thought I would hear you say that.

There's something to be said about just learning how to have a good time.

Driven Zingers!

- Embrace and enjoy Gen Z's desire to win.
- Help them balance their competitive drive with being team players.
- Encourage Gen Zers to admit mistakes and talk about what they can learn from losses.
- Keep one foot on the brake pedal to avoid Gen Z going so fast they make critical mistakes.
- Coach on when to take a step back and let ideas and information percolate.
- Capitalize on Gen Z's willingness to move a product or idea forward quickly.
- Keep Gen Zers learning and growing rapidly to avoid losing them.
- Provide benefits that focus on health and fitness.
- Put Gen Z to work as protectors of privacy, but coach on how and when to share and collaborate.
- Make sure to offer enough private as well as shared space in the workplace.

CONCLUSION

Dad, I don't think we should have a conclusion.

C'mon, Jonah. It's the last chapter. Don't stop now, we're so close.

I'm serious. If we did this right, then there shouldn't be a lot more to say.

Look. You already asked me to go to the publisher to see about skipping the intro. We lost that one. No way am I asking to blow off the conclusion.

Hey, I stand by that one. Intros in books are like manuals. No one reads them.

Fine, but it's professional to have some sort of wrap-up. Maybe the top things to remember?

That sounds soooo boring. Plus we've said that. A lot. If readers don't have a good feel for Gen Z by now, a conclusion's not going to do it.

Okay, but I think we both agree we are on a mission to start a dialogue about your generation. Seventy-two million of you are just about to flood into the workplace and yet no one seems to be getting a jump on this. Don't you think we need some call to action?

You're probably right. Let's ask our readers to share what they now know about Gen Z.

I like it. What else?

Nothing. Keep it simple and to our mission—to pioneer a dialogue about Gen Z at work. Our readers have made the effort to learn about Gen Z and now we ask them to go out and spread the word.

A new generation is starting to hit the workforce, yet no one seems to be talking about it. Until now.

We need your help in pioneering the dialogue about Gen Z. As we said in the introduction, often when we introduce the dialogue about Gen Z hitting the workplace, most of the faces look shocked, mad, exhausted, or confused. They rarely look excited. I have to believe you will encounter the same reaction. But hopefully, as you do share what you now know about Gen Z, most faces will go from mad, exhausted, or confused to relieved, excited, and definitely intrigued. That's been my favorite part of this journey. People will take your lead and if you show some excitement about our arrival at work, they will follow.

Nothing can stop the arrival of a new generation, so why not be proactive rather than wait for costly collisions and be forced into reactive mode?

Obviously you have an open mind about a new generation; otherwise you wouldn't have made it to the conclusion of our book. Ideally, now that you have a baseline understanding of Gen Z, you too are excited about them or at least interested. I truly believe that Gen Z has the potential to light the world of work on fire . . . in a good way. Will there be challenges? You bet! Big ones! However, their potential far outweighs any looming gaps. But again, only if we have an open mind and harness this potential.

How do we do that? As Jonah said . . . help us pioneer the dialogue about Gen Z. Go talk with . . .

Your HR department. The time to explore changes is now. Could your company imagine multiple career paths at the same time? How about letting employees come up with their own job titles? What does the company think about side hustles? The message isn't that we need to start from scratch. It's more about you giving a heads-up about what is known to be on the horizon and where you can anticipate both opportunities and challenges.

Start conversations now with recruiters. These folks are the eyes and ears on the front lines of Gen Z hitting the workplace. I remember that as Millennials started to show up they said to us, "Wow. I'm used to being the one to ask all of the questions. Something is changing." They were right. A vocal generation was hitting the workplace. Often it was the recruiters who were able to spot a trend. What are they noticing as they hit college campuses or job fairs?

It's not too early to talk to your customers and clients about Gen Z. Starting a dialogue that your clients aren't having, but should be, will certainly position you on the cutting edge. That's not a bad thing. More than that, as they react to what makes Gen Z unique, you can get a read on their fears or concerns and where you might be able to help.

If you have anyone in your network who works in industries such as retail or hospitality, they are no doubt open and ready to talk about Gen Z. They have already been hiring and working with them. Some may be on top of it and can give you insights beyond this book. Others may really be struggling because they assumed they were Millennials and haven't gotten their heads or strategies around a new generation. You can help.

It's always helpful to talk with people who have been there and tried that. Who better than colleges or universities? They have been in the battle as enrollments are down and Gen Z is challenging the way things have always been done. Again, many are on top of it, as we saw in this book. How did they deal with the change? What can you learn from them? At the same time, there are others that are really grappling to figure out what their new value proposition is. Yes . . . we would love if you recommended they read our book. But we would love even more if you offered your insights.

Go talk with teachers! Find one you know or take an extra minute at the next parent-teacher conference to ask them what they are seeing with this generation. What do they predict the gaps will be in the workplace? More than recruiters, retail, hospitality, and even colleges and universities, teachers have had their pulse on Gen Z before anyone else. Teachers like Melissa Kondrick have been some of our best sounding boards. We are grateful not only for what they have been able to share about Gen Z, but also for their role in shaping Gen Z's lives. So many of the positive attributes of Gen Z that we look forward to embracing in our workplaces have been harnessed and celebrated by those who have already been their boss—their teachers.

Talk to your professional networks, colleagues, friends, and family. Next lunch or dinner conversation, throw something out there like, "I've been learning a lot about Gen Z—do you know much about them?" It's fun to listen to the buzz or watch the realization that the babysitter is now old enough to be the new hire. It's even more fun to watch Xers realize that we are now talking about their kids!

On that note, for all of our Gen X readers, we can learn from the Boomers. As they experienced firsthand, many of the dynamics that they embraced with their Millennial children at the dinner table didn't work as well at the conference table. Of course we love our Gen Z kids and think we did a brilliant job of raising them. But we cannot assume that just because we think we've mastered the role of parenting Gen Z at home, we know how to recruit and retain them at the office. Rather than wait for the struggle, start talking now about what it will be like to have your kids or their friends working for and with you. Something tells us you won't be short on words.

We need to talk about Gen Z with Millennials. It is so easy for the rest of us to assume, "Oh, you're young enough. You for sure understand Gen Z." It is even easier for us to forget what it was like. Boomers struggled when Xers showed up. Xers struggled with Millennials. Why would it be any different for Millennials when Gen Z arrives? As mentioned earlier, we are seeing a lot of Millennial fatigue out there. First of all, let's remember, we are the ones talking about them and they didn't give out the participation awards that the rest of us are so quick to make fun of. So many people tell us that they are tired of hearing so much about the Millennials. We mentioned in the introduction that it doesn't bode well for sparking interest in a dialogue about Gen Z. However, it also doesn't bode well for Millennials. They will be the frontline managers of Gen Z. So much of the success of onboarding Gen Z will rely on the Millennials. Their ability to bridge the gaps with Gen Z early on will impact everyone in a company, not just them. As much as we will want to smile and think "payback time" when Millennials come storming into our offices complaining about the new Gen Z recruit, we need to show empathy and we need to help them out. We've all been there. Rather than tell them to suck it up, train them on how to deal with Gen Z. We can't afford fatigue. We need to prepare Millennials to step into management. Have the conversations with Millennials that you wish someone would have had with you.

Now that you've read this book, please talk with the older generations. They will need your help in pulling them along. Trust me, they will not be jumping up and down over the fact that once again they have to look at everything from office space to communication techniques to recruiting to rewards. They will avoid it. The problem is that we all know they can't and odds are many will wait too long. My generation needs as many ambassadors as we can get. We can all agree that the world is continually changing. Before long self-driving cars will be the norm, our society will truly be paperless, and space travel will be more than a bucket list item. Hopefully more diseases can be eradicated and new sources of energy can be utilized. We will have to continue to fight to save our planet, protect ourselves from extreme haters, and not give up on world peace. These changes will require all new ways of doing business. Who better to take the changes on than the future workforce? The reality is that we will be the generation that has no choice but to fight the fight. The reality is also that we can't do it alone. If leaders are resistant to getting to know us, then we won't be set up to succeed. More than our future being in jeopardy, so too will be all the legacies that the other generations have created for us.

Aside from talking to the older generations, I would really hope you talk to us. You've learned by now that we are not Millennials. Continue to get to know what makes Gen Z unique by engaging in conversations. For many Xers, it's a little easier since all you have to do is talk to your kids or their friends. But for others, you may not have as many Gen Zers in your life. But we are still around. My favorite finding from our research is that we prefer face-to-face communication. Take an extra minute to chat with the Gen Zer making your morning latte or mowing your lawn, or maybe with your intern, who you just assumed was a Millennial. Some of my favorite conversations are at the lunch or dinner before a speaking event. Executives are so curious and ask so many questions. They want to know what I like to read, what TV shows I watch, who is my favorite celebrity, what brands I think are cool, what college I want to go to, what apps I use, and so on. I can see their eyes open up and, even better, their minds.

And finally, to any Gen Z readers out there: yes, it is time that the other generations get to know us. However, let's be clear that we have just as much work to do, if not more. Take the time to get to know what makes Traditionalists, Boomers, Xers, and Millennials tick. As much as I love when executives show interest in me and my generation, I get way more out of learning about them. The questions they ask me can shed a lot of light on who they are as well, from the books they read to the apps they do or do not like. Find out the answers, and why they think the way they do.

This can't all be about us.

ACKNOWLEDGMENTS

From Jonah

Mom. Thank you for always being there for me. Whether it's a ride to snowboarding or helping with homework, you always drop what you are doing to help me. I love our conversations and time we spend together. Best. Mom. Ever!

Ellie and Sadie. You both are awesome sisters. I think it's so great that we get along so well. The two of you are worth bragging about and I hope you know how much I love you.

To the VANTAGE teachers. Mr. Hurrelbrink, Mr. Sill, Mr. Veninga, Mr. Breen, Mrs. Olsen, and Mrs. Lolich. Thank you for helping me develop into who I am today and for supporting this amazing journey I set out on at the beginning of this school year. I am forever grateful.

To all my friends. You guys know who you are, and you know how much you mean to me. Your excitement for this project means everything to me. I love the moments we spend together and can't wait to see what our generation will do.

To Boba, Gramps, Nana, and my late Papa. From family vacations to family dinners I love every second I am with you. Nana, even though you live in Florida and I don't see you as much as I would like, I hope you know how much I love you. And finally, Papa, I could always count on you to make me laugh. I miss you like crazy.

To all the CEOs and leaders who participated in my survey. Thank you for giving some sixteen-year-old a chance to chase a dream. All of your emails were so supportive and encouraging. I loved fielding the survey and think your questions will help a lot of leaders think about Gen Z. I hope to be as successful as all of you someday and I am so thankful that I had the chance to collaborate with each and every one of you.

Dad. You are my best friend. I owe any success I have had to you. I hope you know that I appreciate everything you do for and with me. I truly mean it when I say you are my best friend. From supporting my snowboard career and spending countless hours in the car together to coaching me on how to give a keynote, you're also my best mentor. I am so excited to continue this journey with you and see where it goes.

From David

Sharon. Your patience and support are everything to me. When people compliment Jonah at events, I usually respond with, "He's got a great mom." You're the best partner in life I could ask for and to think that after twenty-two years of marriage it still feels like just the beginning.

Ellie and Sadie. Thank you for being part of my Gen Z lab. So much of what you say or do every day not only makes me excited about your generation, but makes me feel like the luckiest dad in the world. I love you both so much.

Lynne Lancaster. My mentor, friend, and collaborator. I love that you are still with me to bridge generation gaps. Your insights into this project made it all the more powerful and personally special. We were made to collaborate, it never gets old, and it's so exciting to think what is yet to come. Thank you. Thank you. Thank. You.

Mom and Dad. I feel so lucky to have been raised by Traditionalists who have always put family first. As a Gen X parent, I have nothing to rebel against and only role models to emulate. Thank you for setting such an amazing example for me as I try to raise my kids.

Marty and Amy. I really do have the best brother and sister-in-law. Thank you for your strategic and caring eye. You have always helped me see things more clearly. Also thank for giving me two amazing nephews and an incredible niece—Jacob, Zachary, and Ruby.

Eunice, Debs, Roland, Roan, and Rose. Even though we don't see you enough, I always feel your love and support.

Kim Lear and Inlay Insights. The queen of secondary research! Our sessions were legendary and something I always looked forward to. More than the research role, I especially valued your eye for the voice of the Millennials. You do your generation proud.

To my sounding board. John Mik, Rob Ribnick, Dean Phillips, Ellen Luger, Nate Garvis, Dale Engquist, David Ezrilov, David Grossman, David Africano, Dean Salita, David and Jennifer Miller, Randi Levine, Brenda Cassellius, Billy Weisman, Mike Fiterman, Richard Davis, Dan Buettner, Seth Mattison, Zoe Stern, Jeff Linzer, Charlene Briner, Andy Stillman, Aubrey Margolis and Beth Leonard . . . From reading and reacting to the manuscript to always being there for just the right advice. Your support and collaboration make me who I am today. One lucky guy!

Nancy and Keith Alper. Whether it's for business or for pleasure, any time I get to spend with you is priceless.

Eva Haller. You're an amazing mentor to me. I feel so lucky to learn from your legacy every single day.

Geniecast Team. Thanks for being so patient with me during the book-writing process. I am so proud of what we have all built together and look forward to where we are going.

WE. If it weren't for you, I would not have been so immersed in Gen Z and interested in this project. I can honestly say that you are the hardest-working team I have ever worked with. Although not everyone is still there, our work together will last forever. Marc and Craig, you are like brothers to me.

Jonah. You are a dream son. We have been buddies forever and truly have so much fun. Now we get to be business partners. I love watching you interact in the business world. It gives me so much hope for the future. You're going to be successful no matter what you do . . . and I think you will do an amazing job introducing Gen Z. I am so proud of how hard you worked on this book. I love you.

From David and Jonah

Hollis Heimbouch. Thank you for believing in this project from the get-go. You assembled an amazing team. Big shout-out to Jonathan Burnham, Kathy Schneider, Tina Andreadis, Brian Perin, Penny Makras, Cindy Achar, Rachel Elinksky, and Nate Knaebel. It is an honor to collaborate with all of you.

Stephanie Hitchcock. You not only helped us find our voices, but you did an incredible job of preserving them. This book would not have happened without you. Period. Thank you for guiding us through the whole process and making every step of the way so much fun. Best. Editor. Ever.

Sandra Dijkstra. For the past twenty years you've been an amazing agent! Three books later, your vision is still spot-on! Thank you for taking Jonah under your wing.

Jay Jamrog, and the i4cp team. We can have theories or predictions all day long, but without real data to back them up, we don't have a book. Thank you for being an incredible research partner, mentor, and friend.

VANTAGE team. The goal of this book was to capture the voice of Gen Z. You were on the front lines from day one. From the surveys to caucuses to infographics to videos and more—you were all an integral part of the team.

Jeff Erickson. One of the first questions we get asked when we are on the road is if Jonah's school is cool with him missing school. Thanks for believing in this venture from the beginning and being so supportive.

Susan, Erik, Margo, Elizabeth, and the Evans Larson Team. It's one thing for us to find our voice; it's another to know how to share it with others. You are the gateway to our Gen Z community and amazing team members. Thanks for always pushing us to where we need to be and sharing your creative minds.

Bruce Benidt. Lord knows the two of us know how to talk. We can't tell you how much we appreciate your gift of helping us to focus on the right words . . . not the most words. The Iowa Caucus will go down as one of our favorite memories ever.

Nitrous Effect. Your creativity is never ending. Your ability to take our vision, ideas, and goals and turn them into a brand is what has allowed us to go to places we never imagined.

CrossFit SISU. Thank you for helping us let off steam every day and being such an important community in our lives.

BIBLIOGRAPHY

Ault, Susanne. "Survey: YouTube Stars More Popular Than Mainstream Celebs Among U.S. Teens." *Variety,* August 5, 2014. http://variety.com/2014/digital/news/survey-youtube-stars-more-popular-than-mainstream-celebs-among-u-s-teens-1201275245/.

Botsman, Rachel. *What's Mine Is Yours: The Rise of Collaborative Consumption.* New York: HarperCollins, 2010.

Bulk, Beth Snyder. "The iGeneration: There's a Market for That—and It's a Big, Influential One, Too." *Advertising Age,* October 2011. http://adage.com/article/news/igen-influential-peers-household-buying-decisions/230427/.

Centers for Disease Control and Prevention. "Number of Americans with Diabetes Projected to Double or Triple by 2050." October 22, 2010. https://www.cdc.gov/media/pressrel/2010/r101022.html.

———. "Trends in the Parent-Report of Health Care Provider–

Diagnosed and Medicated ADHD: United States, 2003–2011." http://www.cdc.gov/ncbddd/adhd/features/key-findings-adhd72013.html.

———. 2013 National Youth Risk Behavior Survey. http://www.cdc.gov/features/yrbs/

Davidson, Cathy N., *Now You See It: How Technology and Brain Science Will Transform Schools and Business for the 21st Century.* New York: Viking, 2011.

Elmore, Tim. "How Generation Z Differs from Generation Y." August 15, 2014. http://growingleaders.com/blog/generation-z-differs-generation-y/.

Finch, Jeremy. "What Is Generation Z, And What Does It Want?" May 4, 2015. http://www.fastcoexist.com/3045317/what-is-generation-z-and-what-does-it-want.

Gallup and Operation Hope. 2013 Gallup-Hope Index. https://www.operationhope.org/images/uploads/Files/2013gallup hopereport.pdf.

"Help! My Parents Are Millennials." *Time*, October 26, 2015.

Huffington, Arianna. *The Sleep Revolution: Transforming Your Life, One Night at a Time.* New York: Harmony, 2016.

"The Innovative University: What College Presidents Think About Change in American High Education." Research report, *Chronicle of Higher Education*, 2014.

Johnson, Whitney. "Why Today's Teens Are More Entrepreneurial Than Their Parents." *Harvard Business Review*, May 25, 2015. https://hbr.org/2015/05/why-todays-teens-are-more-entrepreneurial-than-their-parents.

JWT Intelligence. "Forward-Looking, Worried About Their Future . . ." April 23, 2012. http://www.slideshare.net/jwtintelligence/

f-external-genz041812–12653599/18-FORWARDLOOKING_WORRIED_ABOUT_THEIR_FUTUREFIGURE.

JWT Intelligence. "Gen Z: Digital in their DNA."

———. Will Paley. "Student: For Gen Z, Digital Connections Trump Money, Music, More." April 27, 2012. https://www.jwtintelligence.com/2012/04/data-point-for-gen-z-digital-connections-trump-money-music-more/.

Kolodny, Lora. "Why a Nonprofit Backs Dropping Out of School." *Wall Street Journal,* December 2013. http://www.wsj.com/articles/SB10001424052702303330204579250142741126468.

Lancaster, Lynne C., and David Stillman. *The M-Factor: How the Millennial Generation Is Rocking the Workplace.* New York: HarperBusiness, 2010.

———. *When Generations Collide.* New York: HarperCollins, 2002.

Magid Generational Strategies, Frank N. Magid Associates. "The First Generation of the Twenty-First Century." http://magid.com/sites/default/files/pdf/MagidPluralistGenerationWhitepaper.pdf.

Millennial Branding. "Gen Y and Gen Z Global Workplace Expectations Study." 2014. http://millennialbranding.com/2014/geny-genz-global-workplace-expectations-study/.

Millennial Branding and Internships.com. "The High School Careers Study." February 3, 2014. http://millennialbranding.com/2014/high-school-careers-study/.

National Center for Education Statistics. "Table 206.10. Number and Percentage of Homeschooled Students Ages 5 through 17 with a Grade Equivalent of Kindergarten through 12th Grade, by Selected Child, Parent, and Household Characteristics:

2003, 2007, and 2012." Accessed June 5, 2016. Nces.ed.gov/programs/digest/d13/tables/dt13_206.10.asp.

Nielsen. "Younger Consumers Endorse Healthy Foods with a Willingness to Pay a Premium." February 4, 2015. http://www.nielsen.com/us/en/insights/news/2015/younger-consumers endorse-healthy-foods-with-a-willingness-to-pay.html.

Northeastern University. "4th Installment of the Innovation Imperative Polling Series: Portrait of Generation Z." http://www.northeastern.edu/innovationsurvey/pdfs/Innovation_Summit_GenZ_Topline_Report.pdf.

———. "Innovation Imperative: Meet Generation Z." http://www.northeastern.edu/news/2014/11/innovation-imperative-meet-generation-z/.

Oeppen, Jim, and James W. Vaupel. "Broken Limits to Life Expectancy." http://www.econ.ku.dk/okocg/VV/VV-Economic%20Growth/articles/artikler-2006/Broken-limits-to-life-expectancy.pdf, as cited in "How Work Will Change When Most of Us Live to 100," Lynda Gratton and Andrew Scott. *Harvard Business Review*, June 27, 2016. https://hbr.org/ 2016/06/how-work-will-change-when-most-of-us-live-to-100.

Pew Charitable Trusts. "Retirement Security Across Generations." May 2013. http://www.pewtrusts.org/~/media/legacy/uploadedfiles/pcs_assets/2013/emprempretirem4051013finalforwebpdf.pdf, p. 4.

Pew Research Center. "The Impact of Digital Tools on Student Writing and How Writing Is Taught in Schools." July 16, 2013. http://www.pewinternet.org/2013/07/16/the-impact-of-digital-tools-on-student-writing-and-how-writing-is-taught-in-schools/.

——. Internet Project Surveys 2000–2014. http://www.pewinternet.org/2014/02/27/part-1-how-the-internet-has-woven-itself-into-american-life/.

——. "More Millennials Living with Family Despite Improved Job Market." 2015. http://www.pewsocialtrends.org/2015/07/29/more-millennials-living-with-family-despite-improved-job-market/#fn-20796–2.

——. "Most Millennials Resist the 'Millennial' Label." September 3, 2015. http://www.people-press.org/2015/09/03/most-millennials-resist-the-millennial-label/.

Pew Research Center, Pew Internet, College Board, and National Writing Project. "How Teens Do Research in the Digital World." November 1, 2012. http://www.pewinternet.org/2012/11/01/how-teens-do-research-in-the-digital-world/.

Piper Jaffray. Taking Stock With Teens Survey. October 14, 2015. http://www.piperjaffray.com/2col.aspx?id=287&releaseid=2097002&title=More+Denim%2C+Netflix+ana+YouTube%3B+Less+Handbags+and+Broadcast+Media%2C+According+to+Survey+of+9%2C400+Teens.

Ritchie, Karen. *Marketing to Generation X*. New York: Lexington Books, 2008.

Robert Half Technology. "Whistle—but Don't Tweet—While You Work." October 6, 2009. http://rht.mediaroom.com/index.php?item=790&s=131.

Rutgers University. "Rutgers' Heldrich Center Study Finds Three in Four Americans Touched Personally by Great Recession." Press release, February 7, 2013. http://news.rutgers.edu/news-releases/2013/february-2013/rutgers-heldrich-cen-20130207#.V1ZXKvkrK02.

Sparks & Honey. "Gen Z 2025: The Final Generation." http://www.slideshare.net/sparksandhoney/gen-z-2025-the-final-generation-preview, slide 13.

———. "Meet Generation Z." June 2014. http://www.slideshare.net/sparksandhoney/generation-z-final-june-17, slide 31.

Stillman, David, Jonah Stillman, and Institute for Corporate Productivity. Gen Z @ Work Survey. Spring 2015.

———. Gen Z @ Work Survey. Fall 2015.

———. Gen Z @ Work Survey. Spring 2016.

Unilever Project Sunlight. "How Children Inspire Sustainable Living." August 2013. https://www.unilever.com/Images/unilever-project-sunlight-white-paper_tcm244–417250_en.pdf.

United States Bureau of Labor Statistics. "Self-employment in the United States." March 2016. http://www.bls.gov/spotlight/2016/self-employment-in-the-united-states/pdf/self-employment-in-the-united-states.pdf.

United States Census Bureau. "2010 Census Shows Multiple-Race Population Grew Faster Than Single-Race Population." September 27, 2012.

INDEX

ABOUT THE AUTHORS

DAVID STILLMAN (Gen Xer) is the coauthor of bestselling books *When Generations Collide* and *The M-Factor: How the Millennial Generation Is Rocking the Workplace.* He has contributed to *Time*, the *Washington Post*, the *New York Times*, and *USA Today*, and has been featured as a generational expert on CNN, CNBC, and the *Today* show. Stillman has been named one of the "200 to Watch" by *Business Journal.*

JONAH STILLMAN (Gen Zer) is a seventeen-year-old high school senior and currently the youngest speaker on the circuit. He was a nationally ranked alpine snowboarder and has served as an ambassador for the international nonprofit WE, traveling to Kenya and Ecuador to build schools. Jonah is excited to be the voice of his generation and offer companies and organizations a heads-up about our next generation gap.